Richard—
all good wishes
Carl Scovel

NEVER FAR FROM HOME

NEVER FAR FROM HOME

Stories from the Radio Pulpit

CARL SCOVEL

Introduced and edited by

RICHARD HIGGINS

SKINNER HOUSE BOOKS
BOSTON

Printed in Canada.

Cover design by Kimberly Glyder.

ISBN 1-55896-459-2

Library of Congress Cataloging-in-Publication Data
Scovel, Carl, 1932-
    Never far from home: stories from the radio pulpit/Carl Scovel.
        p. cm.
    ISBN 1-55896-459-2 (alk. paper)
    1. Sermons, American—20th century. 2. Unitarian Universalist Association—Sermons. I. Title.
Bx 9843.S37N48 2003
252'.09132—dc21   2003050376

5 4 3 2

06 05 04

The essays in this book are adapted from radio talks written and broadcast by Rev. Carl Scovel and copyrighted by King's Chapel. "Tales of My Parish," an audio tape of twelve radio sermons by Carl Scovel, is available from King's Chapel in Boston. For more information, please write to King's Chapel House, 64 Beacon St., Boston, MA 02108.

CONTENTS

FOREWORD

WHATEVER FAITH you may be, or if you have no iden-
tifiable faith but view the world with curiosity, this book
is for you. You will be not only enriched and enlightened
but also entertained by these gemlike story-essays written originally for radio by the Reverend Carl Scovel.

Emerson remarked, "The true preacher can be known
by this, that he deals out to people his life—his life
passed through the fire of thought." For more than a
decade, I had the privilege of hearing Scovel's sermons
from the pulpit of King's Chapel, that historic Boston
church. How much did his words affect me? His remarks
on Christmas Eve 1980 led me back to church and to the
faith of my father after a quarter-century of knee-jerk,
postcollegiate atheism. His sermons, as well as the classes
and workshops he led, drew me to active membership in
that church, one I will always think of with pride and
gratitude as "my" church no matter how far away I live
and in what other sacred places I worship.

The stories you will read here are not usually about
famous saints or the heroes of history's headlines, but

about ordinary, courageous people engaged in what Scovel calls "the common daily struggle to survive, to make sense out of life, and to help one's neighbor." It is Scovel's conviction that "God looks for us through the most unlikely metaphors. Thanks be to God for all the hunters and finders in the world."

And thanks be to God for those who can tell their stories with the grace, understanding, and faith found in these pages.

Dan Wakefield
September, 2003

INTRODUCTION

DESPITE OUR repeated failures, our escapes, and our human tendency to become lost, we are unable to flee God's love. This is Carl Scovel's message. This is puzzling at first, but as the message reasserts itself, it begins to make sense. We simply have to train our perception to recognize that love, Scovel says, and to let ourselves receive it. Easy to say and hard to do, of course, especially for a former Presbyterian reared on Calvinism like Scovel, but you sense that he has gotten the hang of it and that, if we listen, we might as well.

The original medium for these talks was a radio program. We listen to radios in kitchen, bedroom, and car as we transact the daily business of life, cooking, commuting, folding laundry, chatting, and taking out the trash. Scovel would therefore catch his listeners off guard and call us back to the center. His slightly high voice was not mellifluous. You knew it was an amateur's voice, but that made you listen. Then you heard the authority, the depth, the integrity, and sometimes the poetry. The guy could tell a story. It was a no-nonsense, going-to-wrap-this-up-right-on-time kind of voice, and soon you realized that it drew its power from the fact that it yielded its power to God.

Scovel has an indirect way of speaking about what matters, as if taking the advice of a sign he once saw and writes about here. The sign was in an ancient Roman Catholic church in Nazareth near the childhood home of Jesus. The church was always crawling with tourists and pilgrims, and the sign was meant to remind English speakers to refrain from talking. But the translation was off: "No explanations in church," it said.

On a practical level, the warning may have stopped few tongues. But on a poetic and theological level, it states a fact about religion that Scovel knows. Religious truth is a mystery to be experienced, not something to be explained. Accordingly, Scovel does little explaining as he returns over and again to his central theme, our relationship to God. Storytelling, yes; painting word pictures, yes; being led by strange occurrences, dreams, words, charismatic strangers, an unusual clock, and signs (even actual ones), all yes; but persuading, discoursing, explanations, no.

On the lookout for signs of God in a fast-moving, confusing, and yet wonderful world, Scovel ponders the puzzle of how we may know God. Along the way, he indulges in apparent digressions, such as the talks about clip-on bow ties, Sterno cans, and bottles of Pepto Bismal left in church pulpits; why the Tower of Pisa should be allowed to lean; hiking in the mountains; Elvis Presley's religious fantasy in the desert. Scovel comes back to his central theme, but in doing so he takes the advice of the Nazarene church sign—and of Emily Dickinson as well. Tell the truth, she said, but tell it "slant."

The one hundred talks collected in this book were culled from about nine hundred fifty that Scovel wrote for a weekly, five-minute radio program from 1979 to 1999. Scovel, now retired, has been a minister for more than forty-five years, thirty-two of them as pastor of King's Chapel, the historic Unitarian Universalist church on Tremont Street in Boston. He is a liberal Christian who is widely respected for his preaching. The Sunday morning talks on WCRB, a classical radio station near Boston, were aimed at a general audience rather than his own congregation.

With the support of King's Chapel, Scovel took over the program in 1977 from a Unitarian Universalist minister in Cambridge, Ralph Helverson, who had done it for the ten previous years. Bill Cavness, a popular Boston radio personality, recorded an introduction with the King's Chapel bell tolling in the background. Although Scovel then had no experience on the air, he quickly recognized the distance between the pulpit and the radio studio. When he sat down to write a talk, he once told me, "I knew I had four and a half minutes, not twenty." He knew he would be heard, not seen, that he would speak to people in kitchens, cars, offices, and bed, not in church. "I learned to write for the ear," he continued, "and I learned that in four and a half minutes, you can tell one story, draw one picture, or develop one idea. I learned to stick with the short and simple. I tried to leave the listener with a single memory."

The talks address God, blizzards, guns, poetry, marathons, last words, and impossible things before breakfast. In them Scovel reviews the lives or works of poets, mystics, composers, saints, and charlatans. Each week, he received postcards or letters from a few listeners. He heard, he said, from church organists, inventors, Jesuit priests, atheists, evangelical Christians, John Birchers, Buddhists, socialists, people in pain, people full of gratitude, and occasionally a classmate from Oberlin College or someone who, like Scovel, had grown up overseas as the child of missionaries.

Scovel's method was what journalists call "collecting string." As he observed things that might suggest a talk, he would write it on a scrap of paper and file it. It might be something he saw or heard, experienced or read, sometimes something that someone told him. A frozen blue jay, an odd-smelling stranger in church, a hymn of praise in a concentration camp, a family secret brought to light. Over weeks or months, sometimes years, he would add to the folder. Then as inspiration (not to mention the deadline) struck, he would sit down in his chilly study, pull out a folder, cull through its contents, and begin to write.

Reflecting on the talks for the program's twentieth anniversary in 1997, Scovel called himself less an author than a medium. "I don't think them up," he said. "They occur to me. They happen. They are given. Everything that any one of us gives another began as a gift to us."

Scovel is a born storyteller and has a trained religious mind, but the ultimate value of these talks is neither literary or theological. Rather it emerges from Scovel's own spiritual depths, from his wrestling with God. He is ever hungry for a deeper, more authentic, more intimate relationship with God and eager to know what that relationship requires of him in this broken, crazy world.

Scovel approaches that relationship as a Christian, yet he knows that Christianity has not cornered the market on God. In these talks he speaks to people of all faiths and no faith. He is going for the truth, as he sees it, not the brand name. He may not disclose the truth as an insight of his own; he may not even name it, not at first. He prefers to tell it "slant."

Richard Higgins
September, 2003

HOUSEHOLD GODS

HOUSEHOLD GODS

THERE THEY SIT in the old photograph. My grandfather
Carl in suit, vest, and high-button shoes in an armchair,
reading a book. My grandmother Louise, prim and upright
in long silk dress, also reading a book. Between them on
a table sits Aunt Martha. No, not a relative, but a clock,
one of hundreds produced after the Civil War by the
Union Manufacturing Company of Bristol, Connecticut,
and bought in 1870, I'd guess, by my great-grandfather,
Dwight Scovel, a Presbyterian minister in upstate New York.

Aunt Martha is twenty-six inches high, fifteen inches
wide, and five inches deep. She has a tall glass door; the
top half shows the clock face, and the lower half shows
a man under a tree with a guitar at his feet and a church
in the background. It is labeled "View in Italy."

Great-grandfather Dwight took the clock from one
small town manse to another in upstate New York until
he built a house and settled in Clinton, beside Oriskany
Creek. When he died at the age of eighty-five, his son
Carl (the only minister among the children) adopted it
and dubbed it "Aunt Martha."

In 1912 Grandfather Carl took it with him to Cortland, New York, where he served the First Presbyterian Church until his death in 1932. Only a few months after Carl died, his widow, my Grandmother Louise, took it with her to China in 1933 when she came to live with her physician son, Fred, who was my father, and the rest of us in Jining, China. (No, you never heard of this city, and you probably never will again.) Aunt Martha stood in my grandmother's small living room in the small house where she lived near us until she left in the summer of 1941, having heard that war might break out between the United States and Japan.

Dad took the clock at that point, and after December 7, 1941, knowing the Japanese might take our possessions, he hid Aunt Martha in a corner of the attic. We left the house first for an internment camp and later for the United States, but we returned to China after the war. Dad went back to the old house and found Aunt Martha just where he'd left her. He took her to our new digs in the city of Hwaiyuan.

From there Aunt Martha went to Canton in 1948 (I have a photograph of her in the dining room there) and then back to the States (Bath, New York) for two years starting in 1951. In 1953 my folks went to India to run a hospital for six years. On leaving the foreign mission field in 1959, they moved to a modest house overlooking the Hudson River in Stony Point, New York. There Aunt Martha had her longest stay, from 1959 to 1987, almost thirty years.

4

My father died in 1986, and no one was left to wind Aunt Martha in the evening. Our mother had Alzheimer's and eventually went to a nursing home. In that year, 1987, Aunt Martha came to the King's Chapel parsonage on Beacon Street in Boston, where she rests in an alcove halfway up the first floor stairs.

She's come a long way.

My father called her one of his Lares and Penates, and it took me a while to understand that she was one of the movable "gods" of our household. She went with us from place to place, like the Ark of the Covenant with the ancient Hebrews, and she gave us a sense of connection with America as we moved around China and India. If you've spent a lifetime moving, or even if you made but one painful move, you know what I mean.

You may yourself have some Lares and Penates—a vase, an old photograph, treasured books, a set of candlesticks—the locus of divinity. They are your small gods and, like all gods, will crumble or get lost, but while they are yours, they give you the sense of permanence that comes in the long run from the One who does not change or crumble, the Eternal, who is ever there, wherever we are.

BEHIND THE CUP OF TEA

EVERY THANKSGIVING DAY there has been a display of fruits and vegetables on the chancel table of King's Chapel, representing the bounty of the earth, the means of our physical survival. In a special way we give thanks for this on a day appointed by Congress in 1941.

Like the Israelites at their first harvest festivals, like people all over the earth in every time and place, we set aside some of the earth's produce, and we bless God for the seed, the soil, the wind, the sun, the rain, the seasons, for the whole benevolent conspiracy that gives us bread on the table and soup in the pot.

What I want to say beyond this is simple, but sometimes forgotten. We enjoy these gifts of the earth only through the labor and planning of humankind. The fruitful earth feeds us only through the supple hands, the strong backs, and the clear heads of thousands and thousands of men and women, and often children, whom we never see and almost never think of.

In the morning I sit at the window and sip a cup of tea. And then I think of how that cup of tea came to me.

First there was a history, thousands of years of growing, cultivating, and brewing tea. There was the great human tradition that makes possible the enterprise of growing tea. And then there are the people. There is the man with the money and will and vision to buy land, hire overseers, select a crop, consult advisers, seek markets, make the whole thing happen.

Then there are the overseers, the fieldhands—men and women who plant and tend and prune and water the tea plants, pick them, sort them, dry them, load them onto trucks. Then there are truck drivers, stevedores, deckhands, more stevedores, more drivers, warehouse owners, salesmen, shopkeepers, clerks, advertisers, not to mention tea tasters and columnists, and finally the consumers, you and I, who sit at our windows and sip that cup of hot, steaming, fragrant, revivifying Hookwah, Darjeeling, Earl Grey, English breakfast, or just plain Red Rose tea-bag tea. Behind a single cup of tea there is a network of human beings who bring the earth's goodness to us, and they are, therefore, part of that goodness.

All these folk stand behind one cup of tea. Think of all who stand behind a loaf of bread, a bowl of custard, a ham-and-cheese sandwich, not to mention a standing rib roast. They are all there—the men and women who feed us, who bring us earth's goodness and are part of God's plan.

THE LAST TIME
SHE MENTIONED DAD

My FATHER DIED of cardiac arrest on January 8, 1985, and my mother was already getting pretty confused before his death. Strangely, after his funeral she almost never mentioned him. If I asked her directly if she missed Dad, she'd say, almost dutifully, "Oh yes, very much."

With the help of a neighbor, she managed to live alone in their house, but with increasing difficulty. In the fall of 1986, we brought her to Boston and placed her in a residential-care center on South Huntington Avenue. Always a private person, she hated the place. After her initial anger and confusion, she drew more and more into herself. And during this time she never mentioned Dad.

Then on the afternoon of November 25, 1987, I went to visit her and found her watching television, her back to the door. As I came in, she reached out with one hand and asked, "Is it? Is it? Is it. . . ?"

"Is it who, Mom?" I asked.

"Is it Fred?" she replied.

I said, "No, Mom, it's Carl."

"Then where's Fred?" she asked.

"All right," I thought, "she's asked. I'll tell her." I sat down opposite her and said, "He's gone, Mom. Fred has died."

"Died?" she asked. "He's died?"

"He died two years ago, Mom." I said. "He was very sick."

"Is it all over then?" she asked and began to cry, weeping for the first time that I had seen for the man who was her lover, partner, colleague, and companion. I stroked her hair and said almost as if in apology, "He didn't want to go, Mom, but he was very sick. He was in the hospital, sitting up in bed, waiting for breakfast, and then he just died."

"My husband's been dead for two years and I never knew it until now," my mother said. Eventually she stopped crying, and we began to talk about things in the room, but then she asked for Dad again, and again I explained, and again she cried, and again she forgot. That was the last time she ever mentioned Dad.

Soon it was time to go. But as I walked down the long corridor of that institution, I realized that this was the only way Mom could have dealt with Dad's death. Only by forgetting could she live with a death so hard and a loss so huge.

Perhaps God in his mercy sends us forgetfulness so that the great pains do not overwhelm us. But it was good for me, their son, to see that mercy lifted for a moment, and I think that moment was a gift for Mom as well—to feel, however briefly, the loss that comes with love.

ALL SOULS

"How MANY PEOPLE in church today?" someone asked me the other day.

I have a bad memory for figures. I stood for a moment, a little confused, and finally said, "I don't know, maybe a hundred, maybe more." I paused, "Maybe less." I remember feeling that this figure was not impressive, that I did not sound successful.

I walked on, wondering why people so often ask me that question. Do they wonder if I'm including the choir and ushers when I give the count, the assistant minister when I'm feeling desperate? And what does it mean anyway?

Then I started to recall who was in church that day. There was Ned and Syd and Ranne and Elsie, Rudi the head usher, the Danforths, the Eustises, Mac, my wife, the couple from Seattle, the new couple who live in Back Bay—(damn! what's their name?).

And then I began to think of those who were in church twenty-five years ago when I first came to King's Chapel: dear Henry Beal, head usher then and the perfect gentleman, who shook my hand warmly and always walked me down the center aisle to the vestry; Marion Homans, with her short cane, cranky, opinionated, faithful, there every Sunday; Ethel Statler, who lived in a rooming house and sometimes took a swipe at the sexton with her cane, as he walked by. Palfrey Perkins, my predecessor for twenty years in that pulpit, sat in Pew Number 3, and we always looked at each other at some point during the last hymn. He knew what it was like to be standing in the place I now stood.

There were others also gone: Ivor Kilton, the poet and inveterate student, who ran the autoclave at the Angell Memorial Animal Hospital; the poor man with the bewildered look and disheveled hair who would never tell me his name but came every Sunday until one Sunday he wasn't there and we never saw him again; Robert Bradford, governor of this commonwealth for two years and our Senior Warden for thirty; the woman who fled to our parsonage from her abusive husband and later happily remarried; the short, sullen man who smoked two packs a day, loved cats, and died of emphysema; the little girl who died of cancer at the age of six.

And then there's that panoply of ministers and lay leaders who are part of the church's lore: James Freeman and his lay colleague, Senior Warden Thomas Bulfinch; Boston mayor and King's Chapel choirmaster Samuel Eliot; Ephraim Peabody, who carved the lovely little crosses while he was dying of tuberculosis; Frank Peabody and his daughter, Amelia, who lived at 117 Commonwealth Avenue, and each left us a magnificent organ.

And long before King's Chapel was ever thought of, there was John Chrysostom, the golden-tongued bishop of Constantinople who died in exile and who wrote the collect we read at the end of Morning Prayer; Ludwig Beethoven, who wrote the tune for a hymn we often sing; Thomas Taverner, who wrote the psalm setting the choir sang last Sunday; the Israelite prophet Amos, who wrote or spoke the Old Testament lesson; the unknown Boston artisan who carved the dove above the communion table and the English joiner who built the communion table in 1600; Paul Revere, or one of his workers, who fashioned the lovely communion goblet we use, and the men and women and children who have filled this church for 230 years.

My mind was reeling with these thoughts as I reached my destination, a luncheon meeting. It was the Tuesday after the Sunday service in which we celebrate All Souls Day. I was picking my way through the chicken casserole with too much pasta and not enough chicken when my neighbor asked me with a genial smile, "How many did you have in church last Sunday?"

I looked him straight in the eye and said without a flicker of expression, "Thousands."

"Thousands, did you say?"

"Thousands," I replied.

The Epistle lesson for that Sunday had read: "Seeing we are compassed about with so great a cloud of witnesses, let us run with patience the race that is set before us, looking to Jesus the author and finisher of our faith."

That's one reason we need never get too elated or too depressed about the number in church on a given Sunday. The cloud of witnesses keeps us sane and reminds us of the source of our faith and hope.

CHRISTMAS IN BOSTON

CHRISTMAS WAS NO PROBLEM for Bostonians until the first minister of King's Chapel arrived in 1686. On December 25 the year before, Judge Samuel Sewall wrote in his diary, "Carts come to Town and Shops open as is usual . . . blessed be God that no Authority yet compell us to keep it."

One year later on Christmas Day, the Reverend Robert Ratcliffe celebrated Holy Communion for a small gathering of English officers and soldiers, a few Anglican citizens, and the governor. And he did the same in 1687. The Puritan preachers tolerated this for a while, but finally Cotton Mather spoke up at the Thursday Lecture, which fell on Christmas day. He asked his listeners, "Can you in your Conscience think that our Holy Saviour is honoured by Mad Mirth, by Long Eating, by Hard Drinking, by Lewd Gaming, by Rude Revelling, by a Mass fit for none but a Saturn or a Bacchus or the Night of a Mahometan Ramadan?"

The King's Chapel minister replied with a sermon on that same day, printed at the request of the Vestry, which defended Christmas not as a day of feasting and playing, but as a day of prayer and reflection. Of course, a collection was always taken for the poor that day. Despite this solemn and restrained celebration, the Royalist Vestry maddened the Puritans by decking the church in pine boughs on Christmas. In 1732 they paid a pound for them.

Well, so it has gone and so it goes today. We keep the good old custom of Communion on Christmas Day. We deck the church in pine boughs. Our verger greets the arriving worshippers, as did his predecessors. We still take a collection for the poor. The service still begins at 10:00 in the morning as it did in 1756, when we celebrated Christmas in our present sanctuary for the first time.

We hear the Christmas lessons, we sing the carols, and the minister still preaches. On this coming Christmas I'm going to tell how Charles Dickens came to write his famous work *A Christmas Carol* and what happened afterward. As usual, we'll hold two services on Christmas Eve, first the children's pageant and later the service of lessons and carols adapted from the celebration at King's College, Cambridge.

Christmas as Christ's Mass is still important to us. Some of our people make much of it and some do very little. Some of our people have homes filled with family; some will spend the day alone. Some will buy many gifts and some may get none. But the ceremonies of this day will remind us all that Christ came to save us from sadness and selfishness, and we will try to receive that message as best we can.

DAD, A BULLET
AND A MIRACLE

WHAT IS A MIRACLE? Jesus breaking bread and feeding the five thousand? Or touching the blind man's eyes and giving him sight? Or speaking to the storm and calming the waves on the Galilean sea? Well, that's one kind of miracle.

Ralph Waldo Emerson didn't like that a bit. He called that kind of miracle a monster. "It is not one with the blowing clover or the falling rain," he said. For Emerson the world of nature was miracle enough, and humankind the greatest miracle of all. And so the argument has gone: Which is the true miracle, Nature or supernature?

I don't propose to settle the miracle question. It will be going on long after I have left this globe. But let me tell you a story, a true one. I know for it happened to my father.

In the summer of 1938, our family was living in northern China, which had recently been invaded and occupied by the Japanese army. Guards were placed all over the city, and one was stationed at the entrance to the hospital where my father, a physician and a missionary, worked. Most of the guards were decent enough, but the guard at the hospital was a particularly unpleasant customer, all the worse when he drank, which he often did on duty.

One day my father went to the hospital after lunch and found the guard in a furious state, drunk and unwilling to admit anyone, including a group of nurses who were due to start work.

After trying unsuccessfully to reason with him, my father pushed by him and started to walk down the long path to the hospital. The guard turned, pointed his rifle, and fired. The bullet went through the small of my father's back, and he fell on the path. As he lay there, he could hear the guard walking up the path behind him, could hear the click of the bolt as he reloaded his rifle, could hear the silence as he stood and aimed, could even hear the tick of the trigger as the guard squeezed it, but not the explosion. For the gun jammed.

For some reason known only to God, or possibly, the manufacturer, something in the action of that rifle stuck, and the gun would not fire—not even when the guard squeezed the trigger again and again. He wandered unsteadily back to his post, and my father, weak with the wound and relief, walked into the hospital, said "I've been shot" to a nurse, and took a bed.

My mother heard the shot. Our gatekeeper's wife rushed into the house wailing that my father had been killed. The gatekeeper brought her to the hospital, and she found Dad lying in a small pool of blood in a ward. "How are you?" she asked. "I don't know," he said, "and we won't for a few hours." The external bleeding had stopped, but no one knew if his internal organs had been damaged. He might need surgery, and at that time he was the only surgeon around.

My mother sent a friend with a motorcycle to the nearest mission hospital twenty miles away. Then she went back to the house and collected the three of us (I was the second born) and took us to the hospital to show us that our father was alive.

I remember walking into his room (he'd been moved by now) and seeing the man who was the closest thing to God in my life lying pale and still under the blood-stained sheets. And I remember my father's mother, who had arrived when we did, coming into the room and saying to Dad with her splendid Victorian confidence, "Fred, you're going to be all right."

He was, thank God. He survived the shot, the infection, the crowds of visitors who flocked first to the hospital and then to the house. He returned to his work and another fifty years of life, most of them good.

We remember that incident as one sign of God's care of our family during the tempestuous years of war and revolution in China.

What is a miracle? George Bernard Shaw called a miracle "an event which creates faith." It was a miracle for us. There may be miracles for you.

A FLASH FROM A DIMMING LIGHT

SHE SITS IMMOBILE while I feed her. Ground hamburger, pureed peas, mashed potatoes, strained fruits, puddings, and her favorites—chocolate milk and ice cream. She takes them all from the child-sized, plastic-covered spoon with which I ladle them into her mouth. She makes no response to the food or to me until she's had enough. Then she clenches her teeth and purses her lips, and I know the meal is over. Sometimes she goes to sleep as I feed her.

She was once a bright, opinionated, articulate woman, who began her paid career as a writer at the age of fifty-five and, in the next ten years, produced a dozen books and more articles and reports than her employers could use. In her spare hours, and they were few, she continued to write the works of her first love, poetry.

She was a tough, highly motivating mother who raised six children and was for thirty years her husband's full-time colleague in the mission field. Now she sits in silence, unmoved, unmoving. I sometimes think of her as the Great Stone Face.

I also think of her as a house that was once the center of our neighborhood. The doors were open, people spilled in and out, cars filled the driveway, and the well-cut lawn was edged with bright flowers. Then over the next five years, the doors were shut, the windows closed, and the shades drawn. The grass began to grow tall and ragged on the lawn, and the flowers went to seed. The drive was empty now, and no one answered the phone or door. At night, you never saw a light inside. Yet all the time, I had an eerie sense that someone might still be living there. I thought they heard the phone and doorbell but never moved from where they sat. Every now and then, I went to the front door and rang the bell, and every time I waited for an answer that never came.

On my last visit to my mother, I finished feeding her lunch, stood up, kissed her, and said, "Goodbye, love, I gotta' go. I love you." Staring straight ahead, she said quite audibly and quite distinctly, "Yes." And then she smiled. I was surprised. Here for a moment was a faint suggestion of the woman I'd known. It was as if in that abandoned house, someone had raised the shade and waved to those of us standing on the lawn. Yes, there was life in there, reaching out to us.

Someone said, "The greatest distance in the world is between two minds." If so, then it's a miracle when the space is bridged, however briefly, by a word or a smile.

Maybe that's a metaphor for God, who seems so often distant and then in one quick moment reminds us that he or she is there.

GOODBYE TO UNCLE LEONARD

MY UNCLE LEONARD was no success by this world's standards. After graduating from high school in Mechanicsville, New York, he worked as a clerk in a grocery store and married my Aunt Geneva much against her parents' wishes. Later he became a brakeman for the Boston and Albany Railroad and worked in the switchyards for the rest of his life. During the war they ran an all-night coffee and sandwich shop in the middle of the yards.

They raised six children, who produced over forty grandchildren, and retired to a small house in Clifton Park, New York. He played golf and enjoyed his family until he got throat cancer and died in the Albany Medical Center on March 29, 1980. The Mechanicsville paper gave him a small obit, right for a working stiff, an ordinary man.

My wife and I had been out of touch with the Mechanicsville side of the family, but when we heard of his death, we knew we had to be there. We got up early and arrived at Corpus Christi Church in Clifton Park just before the requiem mass began.

It was Holy Week, and the priest appeared in a white cassock and green stole. He went to the back of the church to meet the white-draped casket and to sprinkle holy water on it as a sign of Uncle Leonard's baptism as an infant. Then as a soloist sang a simple chant, he preceded the casket as it was rolled down the center aisle to the front of the church.

Through these simple actions, I began to see that in the church community, my Uncle Leonard wasn't just anybody. He was somebody. He was part of this church, a brother to its members, and a child of God. The priest communicated this with his simple celebration of the funeral mass.

At the homily he said, "Easter came early to our brother Leonard. And while it may seem strange in Holy Week to come to church and see the Paschal candle lit and the priest wearing his Easter vestments, it's right for this occasion. We Christians believe that death is Passover, a passing over from life through death to life eternal. And so it has been with our brother Leonard. We are grieved at his death, but we do not grieve without hope. In a few days we will celebrate Christ's resurrection, and in his resurrection we look forward to our own, to our passover, our passing over from life through death to life eternal." His words were simple, clear, and memorable. I even remember the direct and undramatic way in which he spoke, without effort or affectation, because nothing like that was needed to tell the truth of what he had to say. The priest spoke of Uncle Leonard with respect not because he was a big man in the community, but because he was a child of God, like us. Here in this church we were sons and daughters of a king, and though we forget and though the world does not see it, none of us can lose our lineage.

We left the church, and a line of over twenty cars drove to the cemetery on the hill overlooking the Hudson River and the railroad yards where Uncle Leonard worked. The priest said a blessing, wafted incense over the grave, and threw a handful of dirt onto the casket. Then we said goodbye and went back to the house for drinks and jokes and talk and more food than we could ever eat.

But I'll not forget that day nor the message of the Christian church that we celebrate each death as an Easter, each dying as a living, each soul, no matter how poor or sinful, as the child of royalty. At its best, the church treats people as beings of eternal worth, no less at their dying than at their birth, no less during their failures than during their successes, no less in their sins than in their virtue, no less for one than for another.

I'm grateful to the wise and simple priest at Corpus Christi Church in Clifton Park, New York, who taught me a little more of my own faith and made Easter come a little earlier for all of us who gathered there on that Monday in Holy Week 1982.

ADVENT

If you go to Catholic, Lutheran, or Episcopal services in Advent, you'll see that the priest wears a purple stole, just as he or she wears in Lent. That's not a coincidence. Advent is, traditionally, a season of penitence as well as preparation, or rather, a season of preparation by way of penitence. Christ is coming, to be sure, but whether with blessings or judgment, we can't be sure.

That's why we sing the somber "O come, O come, Emmanuel," and in the gospel lessons we meet the warning figure of John the Baptist on the first two Sundays. We hear the story of the fig tree, cursed because it bore no fruit. And on the first Sunday of Advent (Year B) we hear Isaiah's cry to Yahweh: "O that you would tear the heavens open and come down, so that the earth might shake at your presence . . . and the nations might tremble before you."

Advent, a season of penitence, is only four weeks away, and I have a suggestion for you. Why not give up something for Advent? Why not make less of the season of excess? And why not do it, not to make life harder for you, but to make it easier?

For example, some years ago I gave up sending out Christmas cards. Every year I either had to send out a batch to all my friends or face the equally unpleasant prospect of deciding who should get them and who should not. So I bagged it altogether. Last August we sent out a family letter and got a surprising number of responses, perhaps because people had time to answer. So that's one way to lighten the load.

Now how about Christmas presents? Now there's a tough one. In some countries only the children get presents. How about giving only one gift each? Or eliminating the nieces and nephews from the list? Are you listening, family? Some people enjoy making their own gifts and trade a shopping expedition in crowded stores for a baking or cooking or jam-making or knitting or carpentry project in their own kitchen, sewing room, or shop, perhaps listening to favorite Christmas music. If that would be a pleasure, why not? If it's a pain, spare yourself.

What else might you give up? Parties. Some you want to attend. Some you'll have to attend. Or do you? Must Advent be the season of social duty? Is that inevitable? Could you give yourself a break? Fewer celebrations might help you celebrate the more.

Now is the time to at least think about it, if it seems right to you. You may love the crowds and the push and the lists and the phone calls and the soirees, and if so, forget this talk.

But for those of you who need a pause in the midst of madness, a moment of calm in the eye of the storm, a sense of perspective in the kaleidoscope of sounds and images, think of Advent as a time of penitence, a time for prayer, or a contemplative book, or a time to feel, as well as to sing "O come, O come Emmanuel, and ransom captured Israel."

JULIA PHELPS,
A GOOD TEACHER

IN OCTOBER OF 1985 I lost as good a friend and colleague as one could ask for, a lovely lady of eighty-nine. Julia Phelps taught the history of art at Harvard, the University of Trent in Canada, and the Radcliffe Seminars, and she took twelve tour groups to Europe, sometimes in the late afternoon dragging a cordon of fainthearted disciples through the Louvre or the Prado with cheer and vigor. She never lectured without slides, of course, and she was as much at home in classical Greece and Rome as in the works of German expressionists of the 1920s and 1930s. Her lectures encompassed painting, drawing, sculpture, architecture, and urban design.

After hearing and seeing her lectures on William Blake and Albrecht Dürer at our own parish house, I realized that Julia was teaching us not to remember dates and data, but how to look at a painting and thus to see the world itself in a different way. That's what an artist does and that's what a good teacher does. They alter the perceptions of their students.

Did you know that the word *theater* comes from the Greek word, *theasthai*, which means to contemplate or observe? When the patrons of the Greek theater went to see the Oedipus plays, such as *Iphigenia in Aulis*, or any of the great tragedies, they did so expecting that they would relearn reality. The act of observing the play was, therefore, a religious act. They were seeing again the way things really are.

Julia helped people do that. When she showed the slides of Paul Klee's works, beginning with his early, clearly representational paintings, then continuing with his more abstract works, and ending with paintings that were piles of broken shards and fragments, she was showing us through one man's eyes the disintegration of Western civilization into the nightmare of the Third Reich. That was the reality of the 1920s and 1930s.

It occurred to me that it is also the purpose of prayer to teach us to see reality. After we contemplate God's goodness through silence, music, spoken prayers, a moving sermon, a lovely sanctuary, or perhaps through a walk by a lake or the sea, we cannot help but see the world in a different way.

The power of that goodness affects us and enables us to see both good and evil more clearly. I think of a woman like Julia as a seer and a prophetess, someone who envisioned a world beyond our immediate sight.

Three weeks before she died, Julia handed me a copy of an article that she had prepared for *The Encyclopedia of Comparative Iconography*. With characteristic grace she asked me to read it and tell her what I thought. I didn't open the manila envelope until I got on the subway. It was an essay on heaven and began with the question of how to present in visible terms that which is invisible, nonspatial, and indescribable. What a wonderful way to end your life—with an essay on heaven!

Julia and her kind are blessings to us. Thanks be to God.

MEETING RUSSELL

I WAS DRIVING EAST when I saw an old man walking along the shoulder of the road. He was bent over by carrying two old suitcases. Though it was a warm spring day, he wore an overcoat, knitted scarf, and wool hat. I flashed by him, half cursing him under my breath for disturbing my peace of mind. Then I wheeled around, drove back, passed him in the other direction, wheeled around again, and picked him up. He was tanned and must have been sixty.

"Hi, I'm Carl," I said.

"I'm Russell."

He looked at my collar. "Catholic?" he asked.

"No."

"Protestant?"

"Yes."

"Where's your church?"

"Boston."

"Which one?"

"King's Chapel," I said.

"Oh yes, on Tremont Street. They got a radio program, don't they?"

"How do you know?" I asked.

"Oh, I've got a radio. Transistor."

I asked him where he lived.

"On the road."

"You mean, like shelters?" I asked.

"No, on the road." He paused as he looked out the windows. "I spent two winters in the woods off Route 495."

That sounds pretty rough, I thought. "How do you keep from freezing?"

"Plastic. I wrap myself in plastic."

"Doesn't that make you hot?"

He laughed, followed by a cough that turned into a hoarse bark. "I don't worry about being hot. Look," he continued, opening his overcoat, under which I could see a dirty navy blue nylon jacket. "I have two pair of winter long johns, two sweaters, two pants, and two coats. And I ain't hot."

"What's it been like today," I asked.

"Terrible," he said. "The bugs are terrible. I took off all my clothes and rubbed myself with bug stuff, but it didn't do no good. Usually the car exhaust kills 'em, but there's been hardly any cars till you came along 'cause of the detour. So I'm all bitten up."

I asked if I could help him.

"I need a belt. I got two belts, but one of 'em broke, don't know how. Look," he said again, showing me that he had a hiatus hernia. He used a plain trouser belt to hold it in.

31

I gave him five dollars and drove him to the Salvation Army center in Gardner, which was his destination. He said he could buy a belt there. After he got out of the car and took out his suitcases, I could hear him fumbling in his pocket for change. "My Lord," I thought to myself. "I hope he's not going to pay me."

The door of the car was still open. His hand came out of his pocket, and he threw a penny on the floor of the car.

"There's a penny for you," he said. "Good luck."

"Good luck to you," I said and drove off as he bent over his suitcases again. I still have that penny. Sometimes I think of Russell listening to this program from his snow camp somewhere west of Route 495.

So if you're listening to me, I want to say, "Hi there, Russell. You're a tough guy, and I'm glad I met you. You did me more of a favor than I did you. God bless you and thanks."

SIXTY-SIX DRIVING LESSONS
AND FIVE ROAD TESTS

SHE WAS SEVENTY YEARS OLD and had never driven a car, but on July 25, 1975, she went to the Rockland County Driving School and took her first lesson. Her husband had already had heart trouble and might someday be unable to drive. If that happened, she wanted to be the one to do the shopping and take him to the doctor.

So she began the slow and painful process of learning to start, stop, turn, enter traffic, and back up. After five difficult months she took the driving test and flunked it miserably. "Poor engine control, poor steering, and failure to yield the right of way" were reasons given. "I made mistakes I've never made before—ever," she wrote in her diary. "The examiner was a dear gentleman and was not nervous." She took the test a month later and flunked again. "I did everything wrong," she told her diary. "Demonic!"

In August of 1976 she resumed the lessons with the Eaton Driving School and took her third road test in October "with half the world praying for me," she told her diary. Again she failed, for all the previous reasons plus "failure to use caution in approaching another vehicle." "The examiner was raving," she noted.

She took a fourth road test two months later and flunked that one, and on the next day her husband was briefly, though violently, sick, "and me without a license to drive," she wrote.

With a learner's permit she drove home from a Christmas pageant and smashed the garage door. "When will this ever end?" she asked her diary. She took a double driving lesson the next day and parallel parked six times. After three more lessons she took her fifth and final test on January 21, 1977—and passed.

She had spent $860 on sixty-six lessons plus five road tests, and at the age of seventy-one, she had her license. Her husband said, "Good! Now I can have my heart attack." Three years later he did. For several months she was the one who drove to the hospital, supermarket, pharmacy, and church.

When we were children, our mother told us the story of the Scotsman Robert Bruce, defeated by Danish invaders and hiding in a stone hut, who watched a spider swing again and again, uncounted times, until he could stretch the thin thread of an incipient web from one rafter to another. Instructed by the spider's persistence, Robert Bruce left the hut, gathered his men, and defeated the Danes. My mother embodied this story, but it was not just persistence that moved her, but love for the man who was her other self. Do you want to know what love is? It's sixty-six driving lessons and five road tests—and a very tough lady.

MOM'S LAST BLESSING

WE HAD GATHERED at my sister's place in Saranac Lake, New York, for the first reunion since my father's death the year before. My older brother drove my mother there, not a small job because she had become increasingly confused even before his death and had by now been diagnosed with Alzheimer's disease.

It was a good reunion. We sat on the dock and swam and splashed each other, went for motor boat rides, grilled hot dogs, and took more snapshots of each other than we'd know what to do with. Some went jogging, and on the last evening, we drove to the local hotel for a nice dinner in a small function room.

Mom went with the flow and seemed to know what was happening most of the time. After dinner, without warning or announcement, she stood up to make a speech, which I took down verbatim. So here are my mother's words, her last words to all of us together.

"Some of you may not know it, but we are having a party. I don't know if you know what a party is. You could have it here, or you could have it there. You could have it on this side, or you could have it on that side. There are people who are very kind to people who don't get to parties very often. There are people who feel, "Oh, the poor old thing,' and if this poor old thing keeps at it long enough, she'll get parties from other people.

"I do thank you, my dears, very much. I want you all to have as much happiness as I have had by having the children who are the people you are to us. We have been the happiest mother and father that anyone could ever have. I can't hope anything better for you than to have as much happiness as you have given us from the beginning by being the children you are."

At this point Vicky, the youngest, presented her with a small ceramic canary that played "Yellow Bird."

"How beautiful! How lovely! (It kept playing.) How do you make it shut up? (We shut it off.) I don't think anyone has ever had as much happiness and joy from their children as I have had, and I pray and hope that each of you may have the same."

And then she sat down, and by then we were laughing and crying. We knew what she was doing. She was giving us her blessing, her last blessing. However confused she may have been, the intent of her heart was clear, and the blessing continues—in us, in our children and theirs. Thanks be to God.

MY FATHER AND ME

My FATHER was thirty years old when I was born, his second son, his second child. He was a busy man, the director and sole internist for a sixty-bed hospital in a small city in northern China at the end of a railway line the Germans had built inland from the port of Tsingtao.

To his hospital came the rich, the poor, and the middle class, but mostly the poor whose families filled the hospital yard with their improvised housing. This meant my father's work was never finished. He regularly worked seventy- and eighty-hour weeks.

We always had breakfast, lunch, and supper together, and until we were ten years old, he read to us at bedtime— all the Winnie the Pooh, Br'er Rabbit, and Uncle Wiggly stories. Despite this I do not remember feeling close to my father.

In fact, I have no memory of being alone with my father except once, when I was eleven years old. I remember sitting beside him in the dining hall of our internment camp, smelling his sweat after he had finished his stint of pumping water, and eating bread and soup with him, and feeling very proud, very pleased, and safe to be beside him.

I also remember that on the Christmas of 1942 when my parents had no money to buy anything, my father, who then knew hardly which end of a hammer to pick up, made me a hobbyhorse, perhaps the most touching gift I have ever received.

As I write this, it occurs to me that it was not just busy-ness that kept my father from coming close to us, that he also felt uneasy when we came "too close." He didn't know what to do with us at that proximity. He had never been taught that kind of thing by his own parents, who were wonderful people but perhaps somewhat distant as well.

During my adolescence I was away at boarding school and came home only for vacations; after high school I never lived at my parents' home for more than a week. They were posted to India in 1953, and after I finished seminary in 1957, my mother sent me fifteen hundred dollars, half of her inheritance from an uncle who died in California. She asked me to come visit them in India. I spent July and much of August with them at their home and at a hill station in northwestern India—reading, talking, traveling, and living their life, getting to know them in an easy way.

At the end of my visit, my father accompanied me to New Delhi, where we spent the night before my departure. After supper Dad asked me if I would like to go out and have a beer. I said that would be fine. Now Dad and

I had never had a drink together, and Dad had probably not had a drink since he came to New Delhi five years before. I doubt that he had the slightest idea of where to find a beer in New Delhi in the daytime let alone at night, but out we went in search of a beer.

I don't recall the details of that search, but I know we walked many a darkened street with an increasing sense of frustration, and at length Dad, a bit sad and embarrassed, said that perhaps we'd better give it up, and I said fine, and we returned to the guest house.

I don't think Dad even wanted a beer but thought it was the right thing to do with an adult son. His offer was a fumbled but well-intentioned rite of passage, an act whereby he could say to me implicitly, "I am a man, and you are a man, and we both know that now." I am still touched by his intention.

Dad never learned to relax with us or hug us, nor did we learn to be that way with him. But I never doubted his deep affection, his interest in our lives and work, and his concern for our happiness. I still remember that search for a nocturnal beer with a wry smile and gratitude.

ESPECIALLY, MY DEAR, TO YOU

SHE WAS TWENTY-FIVE YEARS OLD and three years out of an Eastern college. He was twenty-six, five years out of a Midwestern school, and one year into his first full-time job. They'd met the year before, eventually took an interest in each other, and began a three-year courtship. She moved to another city. He moved to a suburb. They wrote, they phoned, they visited, and then decided.

They were married in a splendid ceremony, complete with the wedding march from *Lohengrin* and Jeremiah Clarke's trumpet voluntary. Now three children and one grandchild later, three houses, eight graduations, fourteen cases of measles, flu, and pneumonia, seven cars, two hi-fis, one European trip, one China trip, four washing machines, three vacuum cleaners, and over a thousand house guests later, after many lessons, disappointments, discoveries, and recoveries, and after several fallings-in-love again, they now stand in the ranks of the hopelessly married.

They have experienced the ancient truth of Genesis: Man and woman are complements to each other.

Shakespeare put it this way:

> He is the half-part of a blessed man
> Left to be finished by such as she,
> And she a fair divided excellence
> Whose fullness of perfection lies in him.
>
> > (*King John*, Act I, Scene I)

Theodore Parker, a Boston Unitarian minister of the last century wrote,

> It takes years to marry completely two hearts, even of the most loving and well-assorted. A happy wedlock is a long falling in love. Men and women marry fractionally, now a small and then a larger fraction. . . . Such a long and sweet fruit needs a long summer to ripen in and a long winter to season in. But a real and happy marriage is one of those things so handsome that if the sun were, as the Greek poets fabled it, a god, he might stop the world and hold it still now and then to feast his eyes on such a spectacle.

The lines fall easily upon the ear, but the lessons of a long, true marriage come with pain and hard work. Yet, as Parker says, the fruit they bear is lovely and nourishing. So our young friends learned, and so by grace and luck and love and labor, they gained a blessing not granted to all.

SOWING PEACHES

SHE MUST HAVE BEEN four or five years old that summer afternoon when Faith and I were planting in the garden, and she had just finished eating a juicy, dripping peach. She came to me with the pit and said, "Daddy, I want to plant this." I looked dubiously at the candidate for resurrection, and with a wisdom born of too many disappointments, I said, "You can plant that, honey, if you want to, but you know, it probably won't come up."

"But I want to plant it," she said, and I replied, "Okay, honey, but remember what I said."

That was over twenty years ago, and last Saturday afternoon I picked up 427 small peaches beneath the tree that sprang from that single pit and now shades a large portion of the backyard, and there must be another 427 peaches still on the tree. They aren't much to eat, but our last sexton made a very decent jam out of them. So much for the wisdom born of disappointment.

As I was picking up the peaches on Saturday, I thought of the stories that Jesus told about the mustard seed. It occurred to me how well he understood nature.

The key to nature is waste. You've got to waste in order to harvest. Waste ninety-nine seeds for the sake of one that may come up, and when it does come up, the tiny little thing you dropped in the ground is multiplied a hundred times.

Of course, what I need is not peaches, but time—minutes, hours, and days. Time is what I'm short of, and I sometimes imagine being given an occasional week with eight days so that I can catch up on everything. But I know perfectly well that a week later I'd be just as far behind as before.

Dorothy Day's friend Peter Maurin, the French socialist, told her when she was complaining about not having enough time, "To make time, you must sow time." Dorothy Day wrote in her journal, "In other words, throw it away. It must seem madness to throw that first wheat away, but more wheat grew up a hundred fold."

What are you short of? Time? Money? Power? Whatever you need, throw it away. Drop it, toss it, chuck it, lose it. And get ready for a harvest. No, it's not a sure thing. Nothing's sure—neither the stock market nor the Red Sox nor life. The harvest that comes may not be the one you expect. But it might be the one you need.

Sow an hour and reap a year.

Sow a smile and reap a friend.

Sow a prayer and reap a kingdom.

Sow a peach pit and reap 427 peaches for canning, compost, and a sacred lesson.

THE STOLEN INFANT

I LIKE TO THINK that after many years of living together, our family has developed a certain sense of equilibrium, a certain ease with one another. At times, of course, differences arise and, occasionally, an act of outright rebellion. But as the reigning benevolent despot of the King's Chapel parsonage at 63 Beacon Street, I like to think that by and large we get on very well.

I don't pretend that all differences are resolved. For example, we have not yet come to complete agreement on just how warm a house should be. I grew up in a house without central heating and have always felt that a cool house is a healthy house, impervious to colds and conducive to the flow of blood. My daughters do not share that sentiment and at times become articulate upon the point.

Last Christmas, when I refused to turn up the heat high enough to raise a winter's supply of orchids, our younger daughter declaimed, "Behold, a decree went out from Carl Augustus that all the world should be frozen, and each went to her own room to be frozen."

"Nonsense," I returned. "You're much better off here than if you were living in China or Russia."

I don't remember her precise response, but something in her tone of voice suggested that she was not convinced and my word was not final.

That Christmas Eve we held our traditional services of songs and scripture, but I added a small new feature. On the old communion table we placed a crèche—terra cotta figures of Mary, Joseph, and the child cradled in its mother's arms, shepherds, sheep, and kings as well. We had never had a crèche at King's Chapel before, and I wasn't sure how people would take it. I hoped that the muted colors of these terra cotta figures might soften any Puritan objections.

We went through the family service at 4:30, Holy Communion at 6:00, and the big service at 10:30, and I heard nothing but words of appreciation. I was relieved and thought perhaps we'd started a new tradition. I had finished greeting the crowd after the late service when our verger approached me with a worried look and said, "I think you'd better come down to the chancel."

"Why, what's the matter, Tom?" I asked.

"One of the pieces of the crèche has been stolen."

"Which one?" I asked.

"The Christ child," he answered.

"Oh Lord," I thought. "Here we put this out for the first time and . . . argh!"

As we walked down the aisle of the church, I couldn't help wondering who would take such a thing. A drunk?

A nut? An objector? A prankster? We got to the chancel and looked at the crèche, and sure as shooting, the baby was gone. I looked under the table and around the chancel floor. Nothing. Then back to the crèche and I saw the edge of a tiny slip of paper protruding from beneath the figure of Mary. I drew the paper out and found the following message, printed neatly in pencil: "We've got Jesus. Turn up the heat at 63 Beacon Street and you can have Him back for the morning service."

The heat went up at the parsonage, the infant reappeared, and everything returned to normal. Well, not quite. The benevolent despot of 63 Beacon Street sits less certainly upon his throne. That is probably not surprising.

No monarch, indeed no despot, can ever be quite sure of his rule when the child has been born.

LOST AND FOUND

ONE RAINY SPRING DAY, our eldest arrived early at church in order to usher. She had a pair of shiny new boots she had just bought on sale, and she left them in the back pew before going to her duties.

At some point during the morning service, a Tremont Street regular wandered into the church and sat down in that back pew. The head usher joined him there and engaged him in conversation until he decided to leave. The drunk had barely gotten out the door before the head usher saw the boots in the back pew and, assuming they belonged to him, picked them up, rushed out to the sidewalk, and pressed them on a very confused visitor, who knew better than to refuse an offer. He took the boots and left.

After the service our eldest asked the head usher if he had seen her boots. He explained with some embarrassment what had happened. She was not pleased, but decided to return to Jordan Marsh, where the boots were still on sale, to buy another pair.

The head usher and a friend went for lunch to the Parker House, which at that time had a window fronting on Tremont Street. Halfway through lunch the head usher looked out of the window and saw one of our daughter's boots in the gutter across the street and its mate not far away. He ran out of the restaurant and across the street, dodging traffic, and picked up the boots. Then he went straight to a pay phone in the Parker House lobby and called our home to tell Helen not to buy the boots. My wife answered and said that Helen had already left the house, but maybe she could catch her if she called the boot department at Jordan Marsh.

And this is the reason that when our eldest approached the cashier's counter at the Jordan Marsh boot department, the phone rang and the clerk picked it up, listened with a puzzled expression, glanced at Helen, smiled and handed her the phone saying, "It's for you."

"Lost and Found" is one of the oldest and loveliest stories in the world. Whether it's a poor widow finding a lost coin, a child finding a lost kitten, a father finding a lost son, or a young woman receiving her lost boots, the message is constant.

God looks for us through the most unlikely agents and speaks to us through the most unlikely metaphors. Thanks be to God for all the hunters and finders of this world. They are the best sermons in the world.

AFTER HE DIED

I SUPPOSE IT'S STRANGE to think that death and resurrection are two halves of a whole, but that's the only way I can make sense of what Christians call the paschal mystery.

I'll explain it this way. As I look back on the last six months of my Dad's life, I realize that it was hard for us to get close to him because we were worrying so much about his comfort. He was in a hospital (there was no way Mom could care for him at home), and the nearest of us lived three hours away. So we would go to the hospital and talk to the nurses and call up the doctors and do what we could to make sure he was warm and well fed. We worried about his body, which was breaking down, tough for a man who'd been as strong as he.

After he died, his body was suddenly taken from us, and just as suddenly I found that I was feeling very close to my father. I was imagining how he might feel in a situation, remembering how he smiled at certain points in a conversation, recalling his jokes and his quotes, and at times sensing his sadness or puzzlement when family life didn't quite go right. When his body was gone, I came closer to him.

It's a small analogy, but if Christ was ever to become universal, first he had to be delocalized. He had to die. He knew it. He said it: "It is right that I should go away from you, for if I don't, the Holy Spirit will not come to you." The single focus of his wisdom and compassion, concentrated in that one physical being who was Jesus of Nazareth, had to be dispersed, diffused, scattered, if it was ever to become part of the life of the world.

The means of that delocalizing was a painful death, but like the oak that crashes and shatters in the forest, small seeds of the original—small imprints of the whole carried in tiny words and memories, seemingly impotent yet charged with the full power of the original—were picked up by the winds of time and history. They were carried in whirling gusts first around the suburbs of Jerusalem, then by great moving rivers of wind and spirit to the towns of northern Israel, then to the cities of Asia Minor, Greece, Egypt, and Rome, and finally, small groves and later forests of the faithful began to spring up wherever these seeds fell to earth and released their power to that place.

Death and resurrection are like this scattering of the good seed over the great field of the Mediterranean world and eventually the entire world. They are one truth, one mystery, one power, the dying merging into living, the living merging into dying, not by the accidents of nature or history, but by the grace of God.

Some years ago a friend's father died, and the family, following his instructions, told the undertaker to have his body cremated and to scatter his ashes from some windblown point. After doing this the undertaker called my friend's mother and told her he had followed her instructions. Her reply was memorable, "Isn't that wonderful!" she said, "now he is everywhere!"

Christ is risen. Now he is everywhere.

ONE OF YOU

Many years ago there was a monastery that had fallen on hard times. People had grown skeptical, and governments had been harsh, and first the young monks and then the middle-aged monks and finally most of the old monks left. At length only the abbot and four monks lived in the old abbey, and they were all over seventy.

In the woods by the monastery, there was a little hut where the rabbi from a nearby town used to come to pray. One day the abbot went to see him and tell him about the great defection. He told the rabbi that even the five who were left found their faith faltering. The rabbi said, "I know just how it is. It is the same in my town. The spirit has left the people. Almost no one comes to prayers any longer." And so the abbot and the rabbi wept together and prayed together. Before the abbot left, he asked, "So have you nothing to tell me?" The rabbi shook his head, paused, and said, "Perhaps one thing. I can tell you that the Messiah is one of you."

The abbot told this to his four fellow monks, and they were all quite puzzled, wondering what the rabbi could possibly mean. Could the rabbi have been speaking of the abbot? Certainly, he had been the leader for more than a generation. On the other hand, he could have meant Brother Thomas. Now there was a holy man if ever there was one.

He couldn't have meant Brother Eldred. He's very crotchety, but when you think of it, even though he was a thorn in the flesh, he was often right. So maybe the rabbi meant Brother Eldred.

But surely he could not have meant Brother Philip. He was so passive, a real nobody, but then he always seemed to be there just when he was needed. He just appears, as if by magic. Maybe Brother Philip was the Messiah. Now, of course, the rabbi could not have meant me. I'm ordinary. Yet supposing he did? No, that's impossible.

As they considered the rabbi's statement, the old monks began to treat each other with respect on the off-chance that one of them might, in fact, be the Messiah. And when people came to visit the monastery on walks and picnics, they began to notice that the monks had an aura of respect and affection that seemed to radiate from them and fill the monastery and the surrounding grounds with a beautiful spirit. Hardly knowing why, the people began to return, first to play and then to pray. Then they brought their friends.

Then it happened that some of the younger men who came out began to talk to the older monks, and after a while one asked if he might join, and then another, and another. In a few years, the monastery became a thriving order again, and all this thanks to the rabbi's remark and the wonderful thought that he had implanted in the old monks' minds.

So who knows, dear listener, the Messiah whom you seek, the wise man you've been looking for, the Christ who is to come, may already be living in your house, or possibly the one next door. The Messiah may be working at your office, or worshipping with you at your church or synagogue. Or could the Messiah possibly be you?

A World Charged
with Grandeur

A WORLD CHARGED WITH GRANDEUR

LAST SUMMER about twenty-five people from King's Chapel went for a lovely daylong walk through the Zealand Valley in the White Mountains of New Hampshire. The trail wound through pine forests, across bubbling brooks, past beaver dams, by groves of beech and poplar, until we turned off at the Zealand Falls Hut for lunch and time to soak our feet in the pools beside the hut.

This was in the year 1989. Eighty years before, a traveler walked through the same country and upon returning described it as a "dull-brown waste of lifeless, fire-eaten soil and stark white boulders. All about lie great blackened stumps and tangled roots of what were once majestic trees. It is as if some cemetery had been unearthed in that little valley."

Fire was the cause of this devastation, not fire from lightning or spontaneous combustion, but from a logging operation begun in 1880 by a lumber baron named James Everett Henry. The sparks from his locomotives hauling logs from the valley and the sparks from campfires and carelessly discarded cigars started small fires during some very dry summers. Those brush fires grew into major conflagrations that burned out valley and hilltop, in some places destroying the root systems that held the mountainsides in place, and down came landslides and avalanches, which left the valley a scene of chaos.

By 1890 the land was completely logged or burnt. James Everett Henry and his crews left Zealand Valley, and shortly thereafter the New Hampshire forest commissioner walked through the devastation and wrote this report to the state legislature: "As one looks upon the two towering sentinels of fire-blasted rock which mark the opening of this valley, there blazes into his mind in letters of living fire the terrible inscription which Dante placed over the entrance arch to hell—" 'Abandon hope, all ye who enter here.' "

Well, oddly enough, the commissioner, though right in his observations, was a little too pessimistic in his prophecy. Today the valley, bereft of the virgin timber to be sure, is a lovely place, and modest, light-scale logging has begun again.

We sometimes forget that there lies in nature an awesome power of re-creation. We are rightly impressed with man's capacity to wreak havoc, but we should not magnify that power to the extent of forgetting nature's powers of restoration. Man's mindless inclination to destroy is bettered by nature's power to heal and mend itself.

No one knew this better than a nineteenth-century poet, priest, and Latin teacher named Gerard Manley

Hopkins, who saw in the England of Blake's satanic mills the continuing creation that Genesis still sings of. Hopkins testified to that power in his poem "God's Grandeur":

The world is charged with the grandeur of God.
It will flame out, like shining from shook foil;
It gathers to a greatness, like the ooze of oil
Crushed. Why do men then now not wreck his
    rod?
Generations have trod, have trod, have trod;
And all is seared with trade; bleared, smeared
    with toil;
And wears man's smudge, and shares man's smell:
    the soil
Is bare now, nor can foot feel, being shod.

And for all this, nature is never spent;
There lives the dearest freshness deep down
    things;
And though the last lights off the black West
    went
Oh, morning at the brown brink eastward,
    springs—
Because the Holy Ghost over the bent
World broods with warm breast and with ah!
    bright wings.

WHAT A NUMBER MEANS

WILL SOMEONE please tell me, what is the magic about *seven*? There are seven ages of man, seven days in the week, seven pillars of wisdom, seven seas, seven stars in the Pleiades, seven hills in Rome, seven wonders of the world, and seven liberal arts.

In the Old Testament we find seven days in creation, seven years that Jacob labored for Rachel and seven more for Rebecca, seven years of plenty and seven years of famine in the land of Egypt, seven days for blessing the altar and seven sprinklings of blood upon it, seven priests blowing seven trumpets marching seven times around the city of Jericho, seven sons of Job, seven penitential psalms, and a sevenfold heating of Nebuchadnezzar's furnace.

In the New Testament there are seven words from the cross, seven joys of Mary, seven loaves on the hillside, seven baskets of fragments gathered after feeding of the multitude, seven corporal works of mercy (Matthew 25: 35-45), seven gifts of the Holy Spirit, seven spirits that Jesus cast out of Mary Magdalene, and seven deacons appointed by the apostles in the early church.

In the book of Revelation, there are seven beatitudes, seven letters written to seven churches, seven seals on the scroll, seven flaming torches that are God's seven spirits, seven angels blowing seven trumpets announcing seven woes, seven more angels pouring out seven bowls of God's wrath, seven thunders, seven heads on the dragon, and seven powers of God.

In the church there are seven sacraments, seven deadly sins, seven cardinal virtues, seven daily offices, and seven sorrows of the Blessed Virgin Mary.

What is it about seven? It's made up of three and four: three the triangle, four the square; three for the Trinity, four for the gospels. Or it's made up of two and five: two for the twofold nature of Christ and five for the basic Christian symbols. Or it's one for the unity of God and six for the six points of the Eucharist. Or is there no theological sense to seven at all? Does the significance of seven derive from the way we've divided a semilunar month? Or what?

If you think I've got an answer to this question, I will disappoint you, because all I see are these recurrences, and I don't know what to make of them. It may be that aside from the feeling of holiness or wholeness that we have about seven, there may be no more to say. It may be that we can make too much of numbers, especially if we're looking for mathematical certainty. All I can say is that to this observer, seven is not only a number but a symbol, and perhaps because it's inexplicable, it is a symbol of mystery, and therefore a symbol of God.

RESTORED BY LITURGY

IN HIS LIVELY BOOK, *The Man Who Mistook His Wife for a Hat*, neurologist Oliver Sacks describes a man named Jimmy who joined the Navy in 1943, fresh out of high school. He trained as a radio operator, served on submarines until the end of the war in 1945, and then signed on for a twenty-year hitch.

When he got out of the Navy in 1965, at age forty-two, he didn't know what to do with himself. He moved to New York, bounced from job to job, began to drink, and by 1971 was so soaked in liquor that he went out of his mind and was put in Bellevue Hospital. In 1975 he was admitted to the church-run Home for the Aged, where Dr. Sacks worked.

When Dr. Sacks examined Jimmy, he found that the man could remember with perfect clarity everything that had happened up to the summer of 1945, but after that, he could not remember anything, not even what was said to him two or three minutes before. He wandered vacantly around the ward. He could focus on a few things briefly. He could play checkers and tic-tac-toe, tap out Morse code, and type.

He worked in the hospital office, copying records without the faintest understanding of or interest in what he was typing. He seemed to be a lost soul. Once Dr. Sacks asked a nun on the staff, "Do you think he has a soul?" His question angered her, but she only answered, "Watch him in chapel and judge for yourself." Dr. Sacks did as she suggested:

I did so and I was moved . . . impressed because I saw here an intensity of attention that I had never seen in him before or thought him capable of. I watched him kneel and take the Sacrament. I could not doubt the perfect alignment of his spirit with the spirit of the Mass. . . . He was held, absorbed by a feeling . . . he was no longer at the mercy of his faulty memory but was absorbed in an act of his whole being . . . in an organic unity so seamless it could not permit any break. The Sisters were right—he did find his soul there.

And Dr. Sacks noted that once held in spiritual attention, its quietude would persist for a while, and there would be in him a pensiveness and peace we rarely if ever saw during the rest of his life at the Home.

Dr. Sacks's observation rings true, and it tells me that the liturgies of the church, synagogue, mosque, and temple speak to a consciousness deeper and more profound than memory, reason, observation, analysis, or even emotion. They speak to a self lost and forgotten in the world of work, politics, household, and neighborhood.

They speak to a self that is our center, the source of calm and self-acceptance. Without enhancement of that self, however it may happen, we are something less than fully human.

The wise of the world often miss this center. Sometimes it takes lost people like Jimmy to find it and show it to others.

TURN BUT A STONE

WE SNAKE OUR WAY up those too-popular mountain passes—booted, belted, backpacked hikers slowly ascending in single file Mount Washington, Mount Monadnock, Mount Cy, Pike's Peak, Fujiyama, Tai Shan. And what do we see when we arrive at the top?

Well, if it's not socked in by rain, snow, smog, or fog, we'll see the skies above us and the summit around us and the land beneath us. Probably we will also see crowds of other hikers, orange peels, candy wrappers, a lodge with all the amenities of a Burger King, perhaps a car park, train, or museum. We'll see civilization.

You can drive or take a train to the top of Mount Washington, take a peek, get a Coke and a cheeseburger, and be seated all the way up and all the way down. You can go there and see mostly what you see everywhere else. It wasn't always that way. Nor does it have to be that way now if we adopt a certain attitude.

When the first European, Darby Field, ascended Mount Washington in 1642, his Indian guides would go only so far with him. The summit, they believed, was the home of the gods. No mortal belonged there. Field saw plenty of mica but no gods on Washington, nor has any white man since. White men generally do not see gods anywhere. They see minerals and views and other hikers, and when they get to the top of their mountain, they are ready to turn around and go back.

And so we return to the valley as I did via the Boot Spur trail, my favorite—a lonely and misty footpath with cairns and boulders like a Scottish moor. As I stumped down that almost-too-steep-for-me trail, remembering the metropolis on top, I began to think that maybe we go back to the valley to find out why we went up and to look for what we didn't see and couldn't see on top. Perhaps we go back to discover what those two Indian guides knew in 1642 when they would go no farther with Darby Field.

For if we do not believe in God with all our heart and soul and mind, how can we see divinity anywhere? As Francis Thompson puts it

'Tis ye, 'tis your estranged faces,
That miss the many-splendored thing.

Maybe that's why I go back and back to the Eucharist: in the taste of wine and the crusty bread, I sometimes sense the presence missing on the mountaintop.

TAKE A HIKE

WHEN I'VE BEEN under pressure and the pressure is getting to me, I know it's time to get out my boots and my pack and a bag of raisins, and drive my old Volvo north to the land of the Great Spirit and the blackflies and the hundred trails and logging roads that snake their secret ways through the thick green woods up the flanks of the White Mountains. I need to head for a summit where the wind and the light and the view are waiting to welcome the lonely walker who has no other purpose than to be there for an hour or two.

It was cloudy and threatening when I left at 6:00 one morning for such a hike, and rain was promised. I was feeling about as mean as a preacher can feel when he's not been getting as well as giving. I stopped at the Concord Ho-Jo's for a cup of coffee and glanced through the guidebook. "Well," I thought, "I'll climb Hancock. I haven't been there for fourteen years, and it's only ten miles up and back."

I drove up Route 93, turned east on the Kancamagus Highway, and after a couple of misses found the trailhead. I laced up my boots and hoisted my pack and headed into the dark-green wonderland of woods and ferns and mist and a moistness you could almost taste.

The last time I climbed Hancock, I had one thing in mind: to get to the top as fast as I could. At that point in my life, I was bent on climbing the forty-seven mountains over four thousand feet in New Hampshire, and Hancock was number twenty-eight on the list. I don't think I saw a thing on that trip. It wasn't a hike; it was a blitz—up and down, in and out, that's all I cared about.

This trip was different. I sauntered up the trail, not caring if I reached the top or not. I looked at the thousand shades of green in leaf and moss. I drank from streams, indifferent to the perils of *Giardia*, and noted good camping sites. I admired the great rocks dropped in the valley by glaciers centuries before. I munched on my sandwich and raisins and sang little chants to the pebbles on the path and listened to the myriad voices in my mind. And I realized that I wasn't just hiking; I was meditating. I wasn't just walking up a mountain; I was walking into my mind, into that inner world that we all lose touch with when we get too busy attending to people and work.

Just as in sleep, where we must dream to stay sane, so in waking we must stay in touch with that world of intuition and fantasy that we call the unconscious. The church thinks of the unconscious as the realm of the Holy Spirit.

We all must do this—some by reading novels, some by walking on the seashore, some by meditating, some by gardening, some by listening to music, some by going to art galleries, some by daydreaming, some by talking to psychotherapists, some by painting, some by playing.

We all need to be in touch with the world of myth and image, story, mood, and feeling—that world where God speaks to us not in the simple language of fact and morality but in the strange and intricate tongue of vision, emotion, and narrative. This world, too, is divine and needs as much attention from us as the world of numbers, theorems, and headlines. "Where there is no vision, the people perish," says Holy Scripture. Where people lose touch with that world of inner truth, they die from the violence of unchecked reason.

Do not hesitate to take your journey into that strange world in which lies your salvation. God still meets us in strange places, and the joy God offers us we must not deny.

YOU ARE DUST

SOME YEARS AGO I had the strange experience of entering a tomb more than two hundred years old. Our small party almost gasped when the mason broke through the wall of old red brick and made a hole through which we could shine our flashlights into the darkness.

There we saw some thirty plain wood coffins, some piled upon each other and some set on the dirt floor of the vault. Vandals in another century had broken into this vault and torn the tops off some of the coffins looking for gold and jewelry, a vain effort since this was a tomb for paupers. Their bodies were gone, their skeletons dressed in a few rags of decaying cloth. The flesh had long since turned to fine gray dust, and I thought of that verse from Job: "Remember, O man, that you are dust, and to dust you shall return." How insubstantial seemed the flesh that once had worked, drank, danced, slept, made love, and walked the streets that I still walk.

I found the experience of seeing this tomb sad and instructive. I felt the closeness to death and mortality that our fathers and mothers on this earth knew much better than we do. The dead died at home, were bathed and clothed for burial at home, were mourned at home, and only then taken to the church for their last service. The friends and family lowered the body into the grave and shoveled in the dirt. Death and burial were straightforward and simple.

Perhaps in part for that reason, our ancestors faced mortality in a way we find hard to do, and perhaps for the same reason, they found eternity more credible. If our faith today is something less than theirs, it may be due to our ambiguity about death itself.

The church takes death seriously in a way that the secular world cannot. It blesses and buries the dead. It remembers the dead on All Saints and All Souls days. It prays for the dead. It maintains a graveyard, columbarium, or memorial garden. And on Ash Wednesday at the end of the noon service, the priest or pastor invites the people forward to the chancel where they kneel, and there he passes among them and uses ashes to mark each person's forehead with the sign of the cross. To each he says, "Remember that you are dust and to dust you shall return."

It is brief, simple, and powerful, a living reminder of our mortality and what it means to have an end, an end that is somehow our fulfillment. How death could possibly fulfill us boggles our minds, yet that is what the great faiths of the world have told us time and time again.

For this reason we do not perform this ritual hopelessly, but rather with a sense of sober realism and the knowledge that death is a gift as well as a fate, from which God brings goodness. The scriptures say, "The body shall return to the dust as it was and the spirit shall return to God who gave it."

So be it, and Amen.

MAYHEM AND THE MANGER

HER CHRISTMAS CARD came late one year, but I wasn't surprised. I knew that her first year as a parish minister had kept her busy. I enjoyed the P.S.: "Why didn't you warn me about Christmas pageants?"

Why indeed? What can you say about these pageants? What should you say? Is it fair to warn a fledgling minister? They're like war, childbirth, and one microsecond of a holy visitation.

Planning a pageant is pleasant enough. You sit at your desk and write a script. You block out the action. You sketch costumes. You select players, choose the music, and imagine a scene of calm and peace, moving in time and synchronicity like a flowing river.

Then comes the first rehearsal. The river is suddenly a raging torrent. Chaos. Confusion. Misery. The children arrive late, hungry, tired, and distracted. The parents are cross, the choir director exasperated, the janitor furious. The wise men get into a fight with the shepherds—cardboard boxes of "myrrh" clashing with foil-wrapped staffs. Mary slips on the chancel steps and hurts her ankle.

Joseph forgets to turn on the tape recorder in the cradle. And may God help you if in a fit of sentimentality you chose live animals to be at the crèche.

If the first rehearsal was chaos, the second is mayhem—Mary on crutches, the shepherds on the wise men, the choir director on hold, and the janitor on something stronger than herb tea. You survive but realize that what you've been through is closer to the Battle of Borodino than the mythical calm at the manger. Or is that right? Perhaps the stable was bedlam. (Bedlam is the Cockney nickname for a mental hospital in London whose official name was Bethlehem.) In the days of Caesar Augustus there was chaos in Israel: a new census, people on the move, the inns full, townsfolk tense, an occupation army in the streets, and guerrillas in the hills. Rehearsals remind us of reality, remind us that God comes not on a Technicolor screen but in the midst of madness.

It's amazing how well the pageant went on Christmas Eve. True, the shepherds were ogling their friends in the front pews, and Mary looked more pained than peaceful. The junior choir blew the third verse of "O come, little children." An usher dropped a collection plate filled with change. But there was a moment when the lights were turned down and the cast was still and the congregation sang "Silent Night." And for a moment the people felt the peace that God may intend for us.

Strange how this works each year. We look at the kids in the chancel, and we do not see the boy next door dressed in an ill-fitting bathrobe nor our niece wriggling nervously in gilded cardboard wings, but we see these children and ourselves transformed for a moment by the story.

We are the Holy Family—our offspring, our neighbors, our fellow townsfolk. We are the story, and for a moment we know more and better of ourselves than we may in the rest of the year.

Not bad.

A MEAL IN MINIATURE

WHEN WE HEAR a Bible story such as the account of Jesus feeding the five thousand people on a mountainside, we are likely to say "Not possible!" or ask "How could that happen?" The early hearers of this story would not have questioned it. "Of course, it was possible," they'd tell us. "Of course, it happened." But they would contend that the obvious miracle was only the surface of the story. For them, behind the miracle lay mystery, the mystery of how God feeds us.

We are a data-bound generation, the children of digital reality, where everything is reduced to "yes or no," "on or off," "positive or negative." We stay on the surface where things are simple and manageable. We want to know exactly what happened and how.

The early Christians wanted to think of what things meant. They would have caught the story's meaning in four key words. Those four words describe what Jesus did after his disciples had collected five loaves of bread and two dried fish and brought them to him. The story says that he took the bread and the fish and blessed them, he broke them, and he gave them to his disciples to set before the people. The four key words in that narrative are *took*, *blessed*, *broke*, and *gave*. Those are the same words Matthew later uses to describe how Jesus celebrated the Last Supper with his disciples. Again Jesus took the bread, blessed it, broke it, and gave it to his disciples. Now what does this tell us? The use of those four words indicates that the feeding of the five thousand on the hillside was a kind of communion service, a precursor of the Last Supper. Those people may have had only a bite of bread and a taste of fish, but that was enough. It was a symbol of God's care for us, God's promise that he knows what we need and will nourish us. We need not worry.

We say our prayers in the morning, and we go about our work, but God does not forget us. God gives us food, friends, labor, light, air, sunshine, above all grace.

"O Lord, you know how busy we must be this day," prayed Sir Jacob before the battle of Astley, "If we should forget thee, do thou not forget us." And God does not forget us. Even in sleep, even in that small rehearsal for death, God nourishes us through dreams and rest.

Communion became the common Christian liturgy because it is a meal in miniature. And the meal is a symbol of what sustains us in addition to our own work and planning. No one lives without sustenance from sun, wind, rain, cold, and heat, the labor of the harvesters and threshers and bakers and teamsters and shopkeepers, and the grace of God.

HOW CAN I
KEEP FROM SINGING?

THE STORY behind a song sometimes tells the story of a people. About forty years ago the First Unitarian Church in Los Angeles published its own hymnal, a collection entitled *Songs of Faith in Man*, which reflected their humanist philosophy.

I bought a copy, and while playing my way through some of the easier hymns, I came across one that the editor said he got from Pete Seeger, who'd told him it was an old Quaker hymn. Well, that sounded strange to me. I had sat with the Friends on First Day mornings for two years in college, and I knew that mainline Quakers rarely speak and never sing during meeting.

The name of the hymn in question was "How Can I Keep from Singing?" It has a lovely tune, and you can find it now in the Methodist, Disciples, United Church of Christ, and Unitarian Universalist hymnals.

The UCC hymnal tells us that it first appeared in a collection called *Bright Jewels for the Sunday School*, published in 1869. I found it in *Amor Dei*, a Unitarian collection of hymns dated 1901. The tune is pentatonic, which means that you can play it on the black keys of your piano, and the composer is Robert Lowry. The text comes from that prolific author, "Anonymous."

The new United Church of Christ hymnal has the same familiar first verse as appears in the Los Angeles collection, but then reprints the old words that appeared in Bright Jewels. These tell us of God's help on earth and our hope of heaven.

But the UCC hymnal retains one new verse, the third, and the notes tell us that this verse was written in the 1950s by an American, Doris Plenn, during the worst days of the McCarthy mania. During this time many Americans lost their jobs and friends, some fled the country, some went to jail, and all because they were accused by McCarthy and his allies of being Communist sympathizers, party members, and agents. Almost all of these people were tried and found guilty by federal and state committees that were the American equivalent of the British Star Chamber.

Some of us remember what a terrible time this was, and we remember as well the few who stood against the tide of the times: foreign service officials like Owen Lattimore, cartoonists like Walt Kelly, entertainers like Zero Mostel, ministers like Methodist Bishop G. Bromley Oxnam and Don Lothrop of Boston's Community Church, and poets like Doris Plenn.

Plenn wrote another stanza for "How Can I Keep from Singing?" Where did she find the hymn in the 1950s when most hymnologists had never heard of it? I don't know, but she did find it and here is her third verse:

When tyrants tremble sick with fear
And hear their death knells ringing;
When friends rejoice both far and near,
how can I keep from singing?
In prison cell and dungeon vile
our thoughts to them are winging;
When friends by shame are undefiled,
how can I keep from singing?

Thanks be to God for all the saints, including Doris Plenn.

HOW WE READ
THE BOOK OF NATURE

ABOUT FIVE HUNDRED years ago, when seers and scholars were rediscovering the world we call nature, when Galileo was scanning the skies and Leonardo da Vinci was studying the body, and when Renaissance philosophers praised the mind of man, people began to speak of two scriptures—the Bible and the book of nature. And they believed that anyone with reason could read both books and find God in them.

Maybe that was true then, but it's not true now. People read the same Bible and the same book of nature and come out with very different conclusions. For example, Colin Fletcher, the author of *Journey Through Time*, hiked from one end of Grand Canyon National Park to the other. He saw in the rocks that towered above him the story of life and death and felt his own mortality, in his words, "the oppression of my own insignificance." For Fletcher, nature magnified his mortality.

Loren Eiseley, who spent his life studying the records of animal life in bones and fossils, found in the rocks and skeletons beneath his gaze a mystery that stunned his imagination. "Use all the great powers of mind," he says, "and pass backward until you hang . . . in the hydrogen cloud from which the sun was born . . . but the cloud still veils the secret, and if not the cloud, then the nothingness into which the cloud itself may be dissolved. The secret lies in the egg of night. Only along the edges of the field after the frost there are whispers of it." So for Eiseley, nature is mystery.

And then there's Carl Boberg, a Swedish pastor, caught in a thunderstorm in the hills near his native town. Upon returning he wrote the words, now known to us as a familiar hymn.

O Lord my God when I in awesome wonder,
Consider all the worlds Thy hands have made.
I see the stars, I hear the rolling thunder,
Thy power throughout the universe displayed.
Then sings my soul, my savior God, to thee
How great thou art, how great thou art.
Then sings my soul, my savior God to thee,
How great thou art, how great thou art.

For Boberg, nature shows God's mercy.

Three people look at nature—one finds mortality, one finds mystery, and one finds mercy. I think of a proverb: "A tree proves God for one with faith; for one without, a forest will not suffice." We all read the book of nature. But only the eyes of faith see God.

IONESCO,
THE HOLY AGNOSTIC

SOME YEARS AGO my wife and I went to a play written by Eugene Ionesco. During the course of the play, everyone except the hero turned into rhinoceroses. It was quite funny and rather terrifying because you could not help but feel the truth behind this comedy. We could call it by a fancy word, *dehumanization*, but what this means is that in our "progress," we are abandoning what it means to be human.

But I forgot my discomfort, and I didn't think much more about Ionesco. I simply assumed that he was one of those godless French existentialists and left it there.

Many years later in 1985, my daughter, who is teaching and studying French at Boston University, showed me a clipping that reported that Ionesco had come to New York to accept the Ingersoll Prize. In his acceptance speech, he said,

> If I have shown men to be ridiculous, ludicrous, it was in no way out of any desire for comic effect

but rather, difficult as it is during these times of universal spiritual decay, to proclaim the truth. It is still possible, at least, to show what man becomes, or what he may become, when he is cut off from all transcendence, when the notion of metaphysical destiny is lacking in the human heart. That is when "realistic" reality is substituted for the Real, the eternal.

"Holy cats," I thought to myself. "Was I ever wrong about this guy!"

Yes, Ionesco is an agnostic, but he is a holy agnostic, an agnostic who is deeply impressed with the sense of God's absence. The playwright describes how this sense of God's absence affects his own decisiveness. "I am always in the state of waiting for a favorable chance," he says. "Finding myself present in all camps, I choose none of them. I am in the situation of one who would like to win the lottery without having to buy a ticket. I am afraid of choosing badly, so I choose neither religion nor politics. It is precisely the fear of losing that loses you. [You can almost hear the words of Christ.] If grace does not come, that will be a coup de grace. It is the lack of the eternal and the effect of that lack which I proclaim."

In this man I hear an agnostic lamenting our doubt about God's reality. He shows us why we become less human—less wise, less brave, less compassionate, less imaginative. He says it's because we have lost our faith in transcendent reality.

This man makes sense to me. As I see the rise of torture in right-wing, left-wing, and third-world nations, as I see the butchery and massacre and terrorism whether from loaded suitcases or the sky, as I see the violent conviction in one's own absolute rightness, I see an exaltation of ourselves, a loss of humility, a loss of humanity.

I can only conclude with Eugene Ionesco that this is so because we have lost our sense of that reality which sets the boundaries for us. I am grateful for the witness of men and women like Ionesco who cannot believe but want to believe, and who show us the consequences of disbelief. Many men and women have testified to God's living presence. Ionesco offers witness to God by describing his absence.

THE LAND OF THE LIVING

ON A DAY in early June of 1993, I felt inclined to sit on top of a mountain. So I drove up Route 93 into Franconia Notch and hiked up Mount Lafayette through mist and sunshine to the familiar ridge, with its grand views and the company of other hikers.

By midafternoon I was sitting on the top of Haystack, a little south of Lafayette, munching bread and cheese and watching the shadows move across the valleys. A grand panorama of hills and mountains stretched all around me, and it occurred to me that if I took a photograph of this and showed it to a friend, he or she would not see what I am seeing. What my friend would see on a rectangle of photographic paper would be only a tenth or twentieth of what I felt and experienced.

At this point I remembered a verse from the book of Job that says, "I know that my redeemer lives and that he shall stand at the last day upon the earth; and though this body shall be destroyed, yet I shall see God, whom I shall see for myself, mine eyes shall behold, and not as a stranger."

"And not as a stranger." I was not a stranger on that mountaintop. I belonged there by right of my labor and my desire. I wasn't seeing God's glory reflected on a print. I was seeing it myself. The one who looks at the postcard or a video is a stranger. The one who is present is a native. The stranger sees. The native knows.

I find it sad that we have refined the technology of representing reality to such an extent that we now speak of certain technologies as conveying "virtual reality." Virtual but not actual. Technology makes strangers of us all. We have videos of crackling fireplaces, CDs of bird songs, movies about bears and birds and bees, audio-tapes of crashing surf and windswept trees. We have endless, countless hours of tape and film representing mythical and actual lives. And the more technology improves, the stranger we become.

Somehow and in some way we must know God for ourselves. We must become natives in God's world. We must know God in our pains and in our own blessings. We study scripture, we hear stories, we contemplate the saints, we sing the ancient songs, and we do all this for just one reason: to see and know God's presence in the land of the living.

Something of God may appear to you in the waitress who brings you coffee this morning at the diner, or the old man you meet after church, or in a sentence in today's sermon, or in one lovely line in the anthem, or in a story in the morning's paper, or in a chance remark from your child, or in that quick thought that flickered through your mind—which you usually forget, but today you paid attention and remembered.

You may see God for yourself, not as a stranger, but with your own eyes.

LET PISA LEAN

I UNDERSTAND that a team of fourteen scientists has developed a strategy for correcting the five and a half–degree southward tilt of the Tower of Pisa. Their scheme requires sinking steel anchors 130 feet below the surface of the ground to the north of the tower. Then they will fasten these anchors by steel cables to a concrete slab on the surface. By tightening the cables the scientists hope to lower the ground level on the north side of the tower and thus cause the tower to return slowly to an upright position.

The tower of Pisa was built eight hundred years ago. It is 187 feet high, and each year it leans a bit more southward by .039 inches. The top is now sixteen feet off its perpendicular axis. "The margin of safety is very low," says British geologist John Burland.

I have two unsolicited opinions for the scientists and the mayor of Pisa. The first is, "Nothing is forever," but I don't expect them to believe that. The second is "Leave well enough alone." And I don't expect them to believe that either.

Maybe the U.S. Army Corps of Engineers, remembering its own errors, could convince them. Many years ago, the Park Service in Chaco Canyon, New Mexico, called them in to fix a problem. A huge rock, a hundred feet tall and weighing thirty-thousand tons, was leaning over some ancient Anasazi ruins. It must have been leaning that way since at least the eleventh century when the Anasazis built a huge buttress made of dirt and pine logs to keep the rock from falling.

That old Indian-made buttress wasn't good enough for the U.S. Army Corps of Engineers, and so they demolished it, intending to replace it with a modern steel structure. They took down the old buttress, and before they could install its replacement, at exactly 4:32 P.M. on January 21, 1941, the hundred-foot rock fell with a sound that could be heard for miles. The rock destroyed sixty-five rooms in the Anasazi ruin beneath it, and there it lies to this very day.

The rock was going to fall anyway, and the Tower of Pisa will probably fall someday. The problem in the long run is not scientists or mayors or the Park Service or even the Army Corps of Engineers. The problem is finitude.

All things on earth, including marble towers and stone cliffs, disintegrate. The visible world tends toward disintegration, as the second law of thermodynamics reminds us. All physical objects incline toward a simpler state of being, dust or carbon.

We sometimes say carelessly that time is the cause. But time doesn't cause anything. Time is the word we use to describe the process by which the physical world disintegrates. Yet, here's the thing. We'd never wonder about this time or disintegration, and we'd never observe this process. We'd never measure it, reflect on it, or feel sad about it if somewhere in our consciousness we didn't have a sense of something permanent, stable, lasting, possibly even something eternal.

That's why sometimes we need to pray, "Lord thou hast been our dwelling place in all generations; before the mountains or the earth were formed, even from everlasting to everlasting thou art God."

That intuition of the eternal is the plumb line by which we measure all inclinations and disintegration—the tower of Pisa, old rocks, history, ourselves, and maybe time itself.

ANCIENT WAYS

A YEAR AGO I saw Dr. Jim O'Connell being interviewed on television. He's a young doctor, a graduate of Harvard Medical School and a Massachusetts General Hospital residency, who decided to work for a year at the Pine Street Inn, a homeless shelter in Boston, and hasn't left yet. On this program, he was describing how many street people who come to the Inn are used to being alone and don't want anyone to touch them. The medical staff at Pine Street had to find a way to help these people relax so that they could be examined and treated.

At length, a nurse came up with a simple answer. Those who come to the clinic are seated in chairs and asked to take their shoes and socks off. Then the nurse soaks their feet in an antiseptic solution of hot water and Betadine. Once this act of simple hospitality is offered and accepted, the rest is easy.

Isn't it amazing how we rediscover ancient ways? In the days of Jesus, travelers were always offered a foot wash at the local inn or home where they were staying.

Usually the most menial slave did this, but at the Last Supper, Jesus himself washed his disciples' feet. After he finished, he said, "Do you understand what I have done to you? You call me Teacher and Lord and rightly so. But if I, your Teacher and your Lord, have washed your feet, then you should wash each other's feet. For I have set you an example."

Like many other churches on Maundy Thursday, we at King's Chapel performed this act of foot washing as part of our liturgy. If all we did was to copy Christ's actions without any sense of what his followers felt and what he intended, then I doubt we accomplished much. My question as the one officiating was, "What can we learn of our teacher's humility and compassion through this ritual?"

I read about a woman who spent several months in a mental hospital, and she described how one evening an older woman named Evelyn came into the lounge and tried to cut her own toenails but couldn't do it. She was too stiff to reach her own feet. Another woman, usually a rather nasty person, said, "I'll do it, Evelyn." She took the scissors and put Evelyn's feet over some newspapers, carefully cut her nails, and even carried out the parings. The woman who watched this was deeply moved and then realized it was Maundy Thursday.

Now that's a liturgy—symbol and substance. So may it be with you and us.

MUSIC, A NATURAL METAPHOR

Music is the handmaiden of faith. Faith inevitably breaks into singing or whistling, humming or drumming, because true cheerfulness before God is not content with words or deeds of formal piety. It bursts out into oms and alleluias, hymns, cantatas, chants. A Baptist congregation in Houston singing "Abide With Me," a choir in Boston performing Bach's *Magnificat*, Buddhist monks in Bangkok intoning Pali texts, or a rabbi in Tel Aviv chanting the *Av Horachamin*—all these show one great truth: Music is the friend of faith. Even my silent Quaker friends can turn out a very decent hymn in parts.

The reason for this lies in the very nature of music. Music is order in sound and time. It is order in sound, whether the sound is a vibrating elastic surface as in timpani or a vibrating column of air as in an organ or a vibrating string, or a column of air as in the human voice. But music is order in time as well. Conductor Robert Shaw points out that music, unlike painting and sculpture, is not space-art. It is time-art. And time comes in two components: the kind of time that comes back again and again (that's rhythm) and the kind of time that moves in a line (we call that tune or melody). But time in music always describes quality, not quantity. Shaw says, "In music, no two minutes are of equal duration . . . the meaning of a piece is not found in its length. The least pertinent question one can ask of the *Missa Solemnis* is how long it is."

Music is the natural metaphor for life. Life also moves in time with recurring rhythm and linear development. Like music, it fuses many elements into a single event that we experience but never fully understand. We cannot grasp it at any one point, because music, like life, moves constantly forward, and we must move with the tune, experiencing and never completely comprehending—thank God! There is order, and we see that order in part but never in completion.

Music creates a community between composer, performer, and listener through time and history. I never hear Handel's *Messiah* without thinking of all the men and women and children who have listened to that piece and found such loveliness and reassurance in it. And when we sing some of those lovely plainsong melodies from the Middle Ages again in church, I sense a community among those who created music, those who have loved it since, and we who sing it on a given day.

Music is the natural metaphor for life, and that is why it inevitably becomes part of worship, part of our praise of the One from whose wisdom, from whose power comes this magnificent and fragile gift, the gift we know and love and celebrate in word and deed and music.

PAVAROTTI'S GREAT GIFT

As a rule I think that people who do one thing well shouldn't talk about it. Athletes, actors, and authors should be seen and not heard, or at least not heard talking about what they do.

But I have met an exception to this rule, a man with not only a wonderful voice but a wonderful soul as well. I'm thinking of the Italian tenor Luciano Pavarotti. Most of you have probably heard him singing arias or Neapolitan songs or even Christmas carols, as I have, but I've been as moved by the things he's said as by the things he's sung. I recently read an interview with Pavarotti, in which he said,

> Sometimes when I speak, I say 'we' because I mean me and my voice. Absolutely we are two different things, and it must be that way. We are sometimes separate. I realize that this instrument is mine because God gave it to me, and I must treat it with great attention—like a piano or violin or any other instrument. I must care for it as a priest cares for

souls . . . . I am a happy man. I have a wonderful family and a wonderful career. For this I am ever grateful to God. I know that I have something that very few people are blessed with, and for this I consider myself a man of privilege. Someone once said that God kissed my vocal chords. But I think that God kissed my soul to make me enjoy life so much.

I've heard many good singers in my many years in ministry. I've heard people with beautiful voices and splendid training and superb technique, and yet they were dull, dull, dull singers. I've heard them sing Mozart and Schubert, and they might as well have been singing out of the phone book because they didn't understand what they were singing. They had no feeling for it. They had not experienced what the composer and the author experienced. They were persons of small souls and should have stuck to light opera.

Our music director at King's Chapel, Daniel Pinkham, often spoke of people who sing "with intelligence" and that is what I'm talking about. It takes imagination and reflection and total professional commitment to produce the music we hear from a Luciano Pavarotti or a Richard Tucker or a Grace Bumbry or a Joan Sutherland.

A great interpreter of the Bible says that a true genius is one who masters knowledge and technique completely and then moves back into appreciation and feeling, into a "second naiveté," so that one can feel the power of the work.

Jesus spoke of becoming little children again. Perhaps that is one reason that we enjoy Pavarotti. He has mastered the technique and knowledge, and having done that, he sings with the gladness and gratitude of a child.

Such a man is a blessing to us, and a song from him is like a kiss. It makes us glad we are alive.

THEY WILL BE WITNESS

HE WAS PLANTING trees as I drove by his house late one Saturday afternoon in the fall. He was bent over his spade, and a hose still spouting water lay near him on the lawn. Already three or four thin saplings waved in the afternoon breeze, and their cautious movements made me wonder if they'd survive the first big storm.

But he wasn't thinking of such things, standing on a sparse lawn devoid of anything but a cheap stubble of grass. To make construction easy, the bulldozers had leveled everything in this development before they laid out the houses row on row. They left the land looking as if it had been blitzed with defoliants. Now this man was correcting the ravages of the developer, working against the setting sun and the coming darkness.

There was nothing unusual in this scene except that it took place some twenty-five years ago, and the man who planted trees was a black American. The suburbs, including ours, were not friendly places for Americans of color. Only a block away the neighbors had bought a house to keep him from buying it, and I'm pleased to tell you that the cellar flooded in the next big rain. Eventually they sold it at a loss.

This man bought his house with the aid of the Sudbury, Massachusetts, Fair Housing Committee. Now he was planting trees as if to tell his neighbors, "I like this town as much as you do and for the same reasons. I'm going to be around a while; don't count on my leaving."

He's still there. His son and daughter grew up in Sudbury and left for San Antonio and Manhattan. The trees have grown, lovely, tall, and fulsome, and now my friend is raking instead of planting. But that's a small price to pay for planting trees in an unfriendly land. The price of liberty is labor as well as vigilance.

There's more to this story. He worked in an electronics firm most of his life, in an office therefore, and I wonder if planting and raking in his small corner of Eden didn't help him get in touch with the world of green and growing things, the world of warmth and seed-time, harvest and winter, the world that responds to sun and wind, frost and rain, the world that has buried in its dark, moist depths the lessons not learned from books and binoculars, the blessings not found in lectures.

I think of my friend potting about on his land, and I wonder if his digging and watering, his weeding and furrowing, are not part of his prayer, his reaching out through kinship with the earth, to that undying goodness we sense in the touch of dirt, the smell of rotting leaves, the splash of rain, and the ice-cold blanket of snow.

Martin Luther once said that if he heard the world were going to end, he would go out and plant an apple tree. That's what it means to plant—to give the seed to the earth and to trust the goodness that made and sustains this earth, to work good beyond our vision and control.

"If God so clothes the grass of the field . . . will he not much more clothe you, O ye of little faith?"

These trees will stand long after my friend is gone, but they will be his witness, the living symbols of his faith in God, creation, and himself.

OUTSIDE THE FRAME

TWO YEARS AGO our family spent the summer traveling through Europe. I'm still sorting out my memories of that trip.

For example, I still remember our visit to St. Peter's and the Vatican Museum and my increasing irritation as we wandered through the huge warehouses of paintings, sculptures, and objects. It seemed to me that the whole purpose of the architecture and the furnishings in the Vatican was to dazzle the viewer with their size, opulence, and splendor. The experience pointed me more toward the genius of Bernini than the grandeur of God. There it was—centuries of history and tons of art, the best! But the sheer bulk and display depressed me.

Two weeks later we visited Chartres Cathedral just south of Paris. Here was a structure as grand and huge as St. Peter's, but I had an entirely different experience there. The cathedral was lovely yet somehow incomplete. The building did not seem to say "Look at me!" but rather, "Look up, look beyond, follow the lines, see where they go." I remember Chartres because it left me looking.

Others, of course, may react differently to these buildings, but I hope that my point is valid. Good art keeps us looking. Good art succeeds because it suggests reality to us both by what we see in it and what we do not see.

The photographer Eliot Porter wrote, "When you look at a landscape photograph, you don't call it abstract because it implies so much more. What is outside the frame, extending indefinitely on all sides, is implied by what is within it."

I suppose this is also the difference between an interesting person and a bore. An interesting person keeps you thinking and talking of experiences beyond his or her immediate experience; a bore never leaves his own turf.

This may also be the difference between a good person and a saint. A good person is one whom we admire, for any number of qualities or achievements, but we always end up seeing that one person. A saint is more like the photograph Porter was describing. A saint is not so much a good person as one who suggests more than what we immediately see in him or her.

A saint is a window. You can see through her, and what you see are other worlds, dimensions, qualities, and experiences that might, in fact, be yours if you chose. A saint is one who is emptied of self and, therefore, transparent to all the good that comes through him. Saints are willing to be forgotten and that's why they delight us.

There are still saints in this world, not just in stone in St. Peter's or in stained-glass windows in Chartres

Cathedral, but living quietly and unostentatiously next door or miles away. They are the most refreshing people in the world, and when you meet one, you have been touched by God.

A children's hymn puts it:

You can meet them in school, or in lanes, or at sea,
In church, or in trains, or in shops, or at tea.

THE UNEXPECTED CAROL

I CALLED my sister in England on Boxing Day and asked her how their Christmas had gone. "Oh, lovely, quite lovely," she said. "We went to church on Christmas Eve, the late service you know, and we had communion. Well, actually something rather odd happened." And then she told me the following story.

At the Christmas Eve service in Shefford, the vicar celebrates communion at midnight, and the people receive the elements in silence. There is no organ, no choir, no soloist—just silence. Well, on this Christmas Eve service, the people began to go forward for communion when they heard a voice begin to sing, the voice of a man, an amateur—sincere and rather drunk. He was singing "You'll Never Walk Alone," from Rogers and Hammerstein's *Carousel*. Now here's the weird thing. The singer was not in the sanctuary, and he wasn't outside the church singing through the window. His voice was clearly coming from within the church, but he was most definitely not in the church. Was it a miracle? As usual, the truth is more prosaic and comic.

The Anglican church in Shefford sits right next to The Black Swan, a local pub. On Christmas Eve the pub holds a karaoke, that is, an evening of music in which patrons sing accompanied by taped orchestral arrangements. The pub has a collection of tapes, and each patron has a chance to sing one song. Two solid walls separate the pub and the church, and the pub usually closes at 10:00 at night, which is why most evening services at the church proceed uninterrupted.

But on Christmas Eve the town of Shefford permits The Black Swan to stay open until one in the morning, and that is why at the midnight mass the vicar's clipped-on microphone in the Anglican church somehow picked up a radio signal on the pub's amplifier, and the worshippers received Holy Communion to the sound of a soulful drunk singing "You'll never walk alone."

"Well, we could do a lot worse," Dennis, the vicar, told his congregation. "The man's right, you know. We don't ever walk anywhere alone, because Jesus is always walking with us."

You never know when God will speak to you or in what voice. It's only important to listen, watch, be wakeful and ready for the divine surprise, sometimes in the most unlikely incarnations.

THE ELEPHANTS ARE KIN

WHEN WE WERE very young, my parents bought us a series of books written and illustrated by a husband and wife named, as I recall, Maude and Miska Peterskin. I remember two titles, *The Story of Transportation* and *The Story of Coal*. It's the second book that I remember best.

The pictures in this book showed how men descended via crude and dangerous elevators deep into the earth and crawled through shallow tunnels, digging at ceilings and walls of coal, which could fall and crush them at any moment. But in that world beneath the surface of the earth, they were also threatened by the undetectable gasses that crept from the cracks in the walls of those tunnels and could kill a miner without his ever knowing it.

One picture in my book showed a miner working in a tunnel while behind him from the wall hung a small cage holding a canary. The text told me that if the miner turned around and saw that the canary had fainted or died, he would leave the tunnel at once. He knew by the bird's death that deadly gasses were in the air. The bird was his warning. If the bird died, he might die.

This picture came back to me recently as I was reading a newspaper article about some endangered species. As usual, federal bureaucrats could not imagine why anyone would worry about some exotic specimen that didn't make money. How could one species more or less make any difference to the human race, especially when compared with the power or wealth to be created by a dam, a reservoir, or a factory? Why this elitist, liberal obsession with endangered species?

The bureaucrats, as usual, do not understand. The endangered species are our canaries. If they die, we are in danger. If they live, we may live too. It's that simple and that fearful, as I see it.

Churches have been slow to see this truth, but we are slowly coming to recognize our solidarity with all creation. Pope John Paul II acknowledged this during a trip to Canada, when he read a litany, written by a Native American elder, at the fork of the Liard and Mackenzie rivers. Facing the east, he gave thanks for water. Turning north, he gave thanks for fire. Turning to the west, he gave thanks for air. And turning south, he blessed the Great Spirit for all order of creation—for the land, for animals, for plants, for humankind.

In so doing, the pope replicated, through a Native American prayer, God's first great covenant with humankind. God made this covenant with Noah after he and his family and the animals on the ark had survived the terrible storm and flood. Before God set his rainbow in the sky, he said to Noah, "Look, I make my covenant with you and your descendants after you and with every living creature that is with you, the cattle and every beast of the earth with you, as many as came out of the ark."

God makes His first covenant not just with people, but with animals as well. That first covenant symbolizes our unity with all creation.

Leaders who forget this covenant, this history, and this common bond between all living creatures threaten our existence as human beings as well as the existence of animals. Animals are our kindred kind—all of them, elephants and locusts and dogs and cats and cockatoos and canaries. We shall live or die together. Science and the Bible agree on that.

CALLED BACK TO LIFE

CALLED BACK TO LIFE

WILLIAM STYRON'S book *Visible Darkness* includes a vivid depiction of a time in his life when he felt so miserable that he began to plan the ending of his life. He describes wrapping his journal in paper towels, putting it into a Post Raisin Bran box, wrapping the box with Scotch tape, and sticking it into a garbage can that would be emptied the next morning. He says that even as he did this, he felt that his actions were excessively theatrical, that he was staging a slightly ridiculous drama in which he was director, actor, audience, and critic, living in a world entirely cut off from others. He went to his lawyer and rewrote his will and then spent two afternoons trying to compose a letter of farewell. He writes,

> There were too many people to acknowledge, to thank, to bequeath final bouquets. And I couldn't manage the sheer dirge-like solemnity of it. There was something almost comically offensive in the pomposity of anything I wrote. . . . I tore up all my efforts, resolving to go out in silence.

Late one bitterly cold night I sat in the living room bundled up against the chill watching a tape of a movie, and at one point in a scene set in a music conservatory, there came a contralto voice singing a sudden soaring passage from the *Alto Rhapsody* by Brahms. . . . This sound which like all music, indeed like all pleasure, I had been unresponsive to for months, pierced my heart like a dagger and in a flood of swift recollection I thought of all the joys this house had known—the children who rushed through its rooms, the festivals, the love and work, the honestly earned slumber, the voices and the nimble commotion, the perennial tribe of cats and dogs and birds. . . . All this I realized was more than I ever could abandon . . . . I could not commit this desecration on myself. . . . I woke up my wife and on the next day I was admitted to the hospital.

William Styron gives no indication that he is a particularly religious man, and he makes no claims for God or soul or spirit, but I cannot help but believe that God spoke to him through the simple, lovely images of his life and called him back to life.

"See, I have set before you life and death, blessing and curse," says God in the Book of Deuteronomy. "Therefore, choose life, that you and your descendants may live."

Each one of you who read these words has probably at some time or another in your life known the paralyzing touch of despair. If you have not, may you never. But speaking as one who has for two long times in his life endured that hopelessness and has had to accept the discipline of living through it, I say that I believe that God has the power to call us out of that pain into the life that he has promised us at birth. God has the power to give us life again and enable us to walk with our heads held high and our hearts uplifted. I believe that as surely as I believe in sunrise and sunset, rain and harvest.

Hold to that promise in the dark hours, and try anything that works. Reach out to friends. Reach out to God in prayers, especially angry ones. Take walks. Drink tea. Clean the house, and if need be, clean it again. Write in a journal. Call home. Don't call home. Read poems. Find a decent therapist. Use every trick in the book and a few that aren't in the book, and don't forget to call your rabbi, priest, or minister if you think they can help, or at least, pray for you.

And believe that you shall see the goodness of the Lord in the land of the living.

A BAPTISMAL FONT RESURRECTED

SOME YEARS AGO, perhaps in the 1950s, the Unitarians in Springfield, Massachusetts, realized that potential church members were moving to the suburbs, not the inner city. They decided that they'd never get larger if they stayed in their old downtown sanctuary. To be sure, it was a lovely building, built by Henry Hobson Richardson, and had served the church for many a moon, but new members wanted parking space, church school rooms, trees and grass, and the sound of whispering breezes, not the noise of traffic.

It was time to move, and move they did to a church and parish house that they built in nearby Longmeadow. They leveled the old building, but they saved two items from demolition—stained glass windows, which they gave to another church, and a solid stone baptismal font, which nobody wanted.

Unitarians may be iconoclasts, but no one had the heart to throw the old font in the dump or smash it to pieces and use it for fill. But what to do with it? One member had the answer: bury it! Bury it on the new church grounds and mark its location on a map, in case it was ever needed. And that's what they did.

In time, of course, the map was lost, and those who remembered its location died or moved away. Thirty years later, when the Reverend Charlie Slap became the minister, most people had forgotten about the font in the ground.

One spring day soon after his arrival, Charlie was walking the grounds with the sexton when he tripped on a stone protruding from the ground, not a rough field stone, but smooth-cut and squared at the edges. The sexton fetched a pick and shovel, and doggone, the stone seemed to go on and on, until finally, of course, it turned out to be the font. Dead, but it won't stay down! What a resurrection!

The earth throws things up. Every spring my wife and I harvest a crop of stones and boulders from our New Hampshire garden. Every year our city garden yields a bushel of bricks.

And ever since we humans set up living quarters on earth, we've been burying things in the ground in order to get rid of them. And sure as sunrise, the earth tosses them back up into the light—bricks, boulders, bodies, and baptismal fonts. Earth, too, knows Easter and provides a continual resurrection of things we thought we were done with.

Somehow that's good news to me. In my almost sixty years, I've buried memories, hurts, discoveries, and bits of wisdom, old loves, and sometimes new loves, and even—like that scared old steward in the parable—my talents. And again and again in an inexorable resurrection, my God-made psyche throws them out into the light and makes them part of my life again.

I think my psyche, like the earth, knows more than my mind and far more than my reason. My psyche too is part of the resurrection that Christ initiated on that strange and lovely day.

THE DOOR TO MEANING

SOME YEARS AGO I got back in touch with a friend whom I had known as a young man, pre-marriage, pre-grad school, pre-kids, pre-job, and here he was twenty years later with a daughter in college. He wrote me the following lines:

> I turned fifty last year and I've been thinking about that. When you're young, you have the luxury of looking forward. Lack of money, difficulties in school, even the Army, can be endured as temporary inconveniences on the road to a better future. Now I look backward as much as forward and realize that I must live within the limits of my abilities and achievements. I'm reminded of John 21:18: "When you were young, you tightened your belt and walked where you wanted, but when you grow old, you shall hold out your hands and someone else will dress you and will take you whether you want it or not." I'm happy with my life and feel I am still accomplishing things, but

now I must manage my limitations, not overcome them. Perhaps I've finally learned to accept reality and that my best years are really ahead of me.

That's the best reflection on midlife I've ever seen. And notice what happens. At midlife you've reached the crest, the top of the hill, and suddenly you can see the end, both the limits to your life and perhaps the goal of your life.

The Psalmist said, "Lord, make me to know my end, that someday my life must end." That prospect, however fearful, frames our life. It sets what we do within a context and gives it a meaning.

Robert Ingersoll said, "It may be that death gives all there is of worth to life. If those we press and strain against our hearts could never die, it may be love would wither from this earth."

Saint Francis said, "Praise be my Lord for our sister, the death of the body, from which no one escapes." Why praise? First, because without death earth would be hell. But second, because Francis believed with all his heart and soul that death was the door to heaven.

Isn't it strange that the discovery of death can open the way to joy? A friend is dying of cancer, and once she knew the certainty of death, she became poised and clear and focused as I had never seen her before. She spoke of God's presence and God's care for her. She was the minister to those who visited her.

Death is the door to meaning. And we discover it at midlife. Amazing!

BOUND FOR GLORY

I GREW UP in a house beside a small cemetery, a square plot not more than twenty-five yards on a side, bordered on three sides by the windowless gray brick walls of the adjoining buildings and on one side by a low stone railing and an open gate.

I used to wander in that enclosure reading the stones for names and dates. Not a few of the graves were for children younger than myself. Sometimes I sought a corner of that yard where the late sun fell upon the grass and sat on the stone of some child who died before I was ever named. It may sound strange, but I felt peaceful in that place.

I still enjoy graveyards as places to rest and wander. The church that I served in Sudbury was set on the side of a small hill just below the first town cemetery, where the body of many a worthy, many a swain, many a maid, and many a widow lay six feet deep beneath the grass. And when the muddle of my mind grew too much for me to bear, I left my study and walked among the gravestones, returning at least a little more calm if not any wiser.

Of course, when I travel, I seek out cemeteries. In Florence I found the graves of Elizabeth Browning and Theodore Parker in the *Cimiterio Iglesia*. In Prague, the grave of patriot Norbert Capek. In Boston, Hester Prynne's real-life inspiration lay close to the east wall of King's Chapel. But my favorite cemetery is still the churchyard by Lady Saint Mary's in the town of Wareham on the southern coast of England.

I arrived there long before the service began, a bright blue sky above with fluffs of cloud here and there, the chimes ringing noisily from the church tower, and the rows of quiet stones about me. I had a strange presentiment of the resurrection amidst those clanging bells, a momentary fantasy of the earth beginning to churn and billow like a tossing sea, the gravestones rocking first, then toppling, and from the earth the dead emerged, not as they were at burial or even in life, but clothed with light and shining with a radiance far beyond anything this world could offer. It was a strange, brief fantasy, but one filled with joy and with the sense that all of us, not one soul missing, were bound for glory. But that wasn't the end of it.

I had been reading names from the stones, old Saxon and Norman names from the ancient families of Wareham, for this was, after all, a parish church. Then I came to a newer section and saw the names of Wareham's sons who had died in the first Great War and then the second—soldiers, sailors, airmen, members of the merchant marine, fire fighters. And there among the English dead I found strange names from another land:

Otto Possega, Hans Funk, Konrad Koehler, Rudolf Kuebler, Klaus Thiessen, Wolfgang Christoph, and written beneath the names of one of them in German, not in English, "Ein Deutcher Soldat." These were German airmen who had been bombing Bourne and Wareham and London, burning homes and blasting schools and wharves and hospitals and markets.

The people of Wareham had fetched their bodies from the fields and sea and given the corpses of their destroyers a place in their own precious churchyard. Perhaps they did this because they knew in a way far beyond mere articulation that God's love comprehends us all. Their Christian compassion or their English decency or both or their sense of what is proper made my fantasy of the resurrection seem all the more ecstatic and surreal.

Perhaps you see why I can find cemeteries to be places of peace and blessing. After all, the turning point of Christian faith came in a graveyard and some of the earliest services were held in catacombs.

Even now we are promised that the place of death is also the place of resurrection.

RESURRECTION GIVES US LIFE

SOME YEARS AGO a Zen master from Japan visited an American Trappist monastery for an extended stay. The abbot hoped that his monks might learn something about meditation from their visitor.

The visitor was impressed with the devotion of this community and eventually offered to conduct a retreat for residents who were interested. Several monks registered for the retreat, and on the first day of the retreat, the monks were given their koans.

A *koan* is a short verbal puzzle that a teacher gives to his disciple. The disciple meditates in silence on this puzzle, and after a specified time—a day, a week, or a month—he returns to his master and reports his reflections as briefly as he can.

On this occasion the first monk entered the master's room and found him kneeling before two copies of the New Testament, one in English and one in Japanese. The monk sat down before the master and waited. The master said in broken but clear English, "You know, I like Christianity, but . . . ." He paused and glanced down at the books before him, then looked up again. "But," he said, "I would not like it without the resurrection."

The master leaned forward so that his face was quite close to that of the monk. "Show me your resurrection," he said. "That is your koan. Show me your resurrection."

The master might be speaking to all of us. If we are Christians in life more than name, then we must live our faith. I hear many Christians witnessing to their faith, but the tone of their message is anger, fear, or arrogance. You can see them on the screen and have heard them in public parks. It's no surprise that people turn away from them.

The unchurched are not waiting for arguments. They are not waiting for proofs. They are not waiting for admission to our splendid liturgies. They have no interest in dull preaching or preaching that tries not to be dull. And they do not need to be insulted. The unchurched are waiting for one thing: the sight of our transformation by the faith we profess.

We may show our transformation in words, deeds, silence, being, bearing, suffering, but our witnessing must be natural, true, and clear—the evidence that God has in some way touched our lives.

Before I even think of reporting the resurrection, I must have received it. Before I enact it, I must experience it. Before I convince another, I must trust the promise of eternal life. It is not easy to trust God's love. We must give up the illusion of controlling our own lives and the lives of those around us. We must give up the hope that we are somehow in charge.

In order to show the resurrection, we must return to the grave, the cross, the upper room, and the lakeside and meet again the One whose resurrection gives us life. That's where it all begins—with this encounter. And once it has taken place, we can show our resurrection.

THE TOMB IS EMPTY

An Episcopal bishop once told me a story about Easter that has stayed with me for many years. It seems that a fourth grade religious education teacher in the Alabama church that he served was trying to explain the Easter story to her children and told them the story of the empty tomb. Then she gave each of them a plastic shell, the kind that pantyhose used to come in. She asked the children to return next Sunday with something in that shell that reminded them of the empty tomb.

On the next Sunday they opened their eggs. One had a flower, one had a tiny felt bunny, one had a small picture of Jesus. Eventually they came to a boy who was mentally retarded. He was older than most of the children because he had been held back for two years. He knew it and the other children knew it. They were uncomfortable with him and avoided him, occasionally mocking him behind the teacher's back.

When his turn came, he opened his shell and there was nothing inside. The other children snickered. The boy said something rather incoherent, trying to explain his presentation, and the teacher listened carefully to him. Then she looked up to the others and said, "He means the empty tomb." The boy, of course, had gotten it.

Christian faith does not begin with flowers, bunnies, or pictures of Jesus. It begins with emptiness, a tomb without a body. For the empty tomb is the one resurrection story found in all four gospels. In fact, the empty tomb is the one claim in the story that could have been proven right or wrong. You can't argue very well with someone who has had a vision of the risen Christ. They've seen him, and maybe you haven't. But if someone says that the tomb is empty, you need only send one trusted person to inspect the site and see if the report is true.

In all the anti-Christian polemic of the first century, no one ever claimed the body was there. To be sure, some charged that the disciples had stolen the body and reburied it elsewhere. Some claimed that Jesus was drugged, woke up, and walked away. Some claimed that the Romans stole the body to keep the tomb from becoming a martyr's site. But no one seemed to doubt that it was empty.

The empty place is the first site and symbol of Christian faith, an absence rather than a presence, and with that space and absence comes a sense that the world is not as simple as we imagine it. For all its laws and patterns, the world still has surprises.

Who could have guessed that a community of martyrs and witnesses would come out of this tiny ragtag group

of confused, abandoned followers? Who would have guessed that a man who was choked to death on a stake would become the center of a worldwide religion? Who would have guessed that the power of his message lives today?

Who could have guessed what would come out of an empty tomb?

THE GIFT OF FORGIVENESS

"LORD, I KNOW you think we should forgive each other," Peter must have said to Jesus. "But what do we do when we forgive someone and he is not as nice as we are? What if he keeps on sinning against me? How many times should I forgive him? Seven? Or seven times seven?"

"No," said Jesus to Peter, "Seventy times seven. For that's how it is in the kingdom of God."

Peter's answer is not recorded. I'll bet he was thinking, "So who wants to go there?"

If we hear what Jesus says as a rule, we misunderstand him. Jesus did not mean that Peter or we should count offenses right up to the 490th and then let our enemy have it on the 491st. Jesus meant that forgiveness is a way of life. We should forgive always. And what on earth does that mean?

First, we must understand that there are three things that forgiveness is not. It is not denial. When we forgive, we don't forget that we were hurt, that we hurt now, that we may hurt for a long time, perhaps a lifetime. Forgiveness is not denial.

Second, forgiveness is not excusing. It's not being "nice." When we forgive, we don't pretend that the offender is not responsible because of his or her childhood or biology. A human being is responsible. Forgiveness is not excusing.

Third, forgiveness is not forgetting. When we forgive, we do not block the memory, nor do we nourish it. But, no, we do not forget.

What then is forgiveness? That's a hard one to answer, but again as I thought of that discussion, the answer came to me.

Forgiveness is not something we give or do, but something we receive. It is not an action. It's a gift. It comes when we want it and it does not come before.

It is easy to cherish anger and hurt. They give us an identity, however false, and sometimes the wrath and pain feel better than the emptiness, which comes when we surrender them. But we pay a price for indulging our anger. It cripples us. We become paralyzed.

When we forgive, we are freed, not from the hurt, but from the dominating power of the hurt. We are able to give up our anger. The hurt and wrath no longer direct us. However it happens, we are free.

We may still suffer the consequences of the offense, but the offense no longer masters us.

Do you see? Forgiveness comes first for our sake, and then for the sake of the offender, if he or she is penitent. They may not be. They may not know. They may not want to know. But we, we the aggrieved, are free.

JUDAS WHO DIED
WITHOUT MERCY

WHAT HAPPENED TO JUDAS, the man who sold the
secret of his master's hiding place for thirty silver coins?
Matthew says he hung himself. Luke says he bought a
field with the thirty silver coins, and then, when he was
standing on his newly purchased property, his bowels
burst and he died. Mark and John don't say. We don't
know for sure what happened to Judas, but we know
that for centuries, he has been a symbol of betrayal. Call
someone a Judas, and you've made a serious charge.

It might be interesting to think at this point how we
read the resurrection story, specifically, where we see ourselves among the disciples. Are we impetuous Peter,
always opening his mouth and sticking his neck out? Are
we among the majority of the bumbling, well-meaning
ten, never sure what Jesus means, never quite believing
that he'd get killed, falling asleep in the garden and watching his death from a distance? Or are we possibly like
Judas, the idealist, the risk-taker, the one who hoped for
so much from the man who eventually disappointed him?

I'm not sure where I would be among the twelve, but I am learning to face my sins and sinfulness. Somewhere in the last few years, I turned a corner in my life, and I think by now I've earned the right to my regrets. On certain days, at certain moments, when I reflect on my self-indulgent preaching or my pursuit of private goals, I realize that I may be closer to Judas than to Peter.

With my attempts at eloquence, my hope to please others, my wish to prove myself superior, how do I know that I have not betrayed my Lord, as Judas did? How do I know that I am not part of the vast betrayal that weakens the church and denies Christ, at the same time that it pretends to praise him?

Judas is no stranger to me. I recall a clergy meeting where we debated how to deal with a recreant pastor, and at one point in the debate, an aged minister stood up and said, "Young men want justice and old men want mercy." Then he sat down.

Well, Judas wanted mercy, but he dared not ask for it, and therefore he shut himself out of the company of grace. That was his real death, his actual execution—to live and to die, however he died, without mercy, without forgiveness, without repentance, without reconciliation. Thank God we need not live or die like that. If Christ died for us, he died that we might live in grace, repentant and forgiven, able to make amends, able to walk without the leg-irons of guilt or the backpack of fear. Christ died that we might know that there is mercy in this world.

JUDGE SEWALL'S
REPENTANCE

THOSE OF YOU familiar with Arthur Miller's play about the Salem witch trials, *The Crucible* may remember the unhappy role the judges played in those proceedings. They were John Hathorne, John Richards, Waitstill Winthrop, Peter Sergent, Bartholomew Gedney, Thomas Newton and Samuel Sewall, a Boston merchant, judge, author, scholar, and overseer of Harvard College.

Few of those judges had legal training. Most of them were inclined to accept almost any kind of report as evidence. Some of the accused maintained their innocence to the end. Others confessed in hope of gaining a lighter sentence, as indeed they often did, and some defendants accused others. One hundred and fifty people were accused and held in jail. Of that number four died in jail, one five-year-old girl was crazed for the rest of her life, and nineteen were hanged, the last one on September 22, 1692.

There is a sequel to this story that few people know about.

After the trials, Judge Samuel Sewall, desolate from the recent death of two of his children, sat in his home, while his son read the Bible to him. When his son read the twelfth chapter of Matthew, verse 7, "If you had known what this means, I will have mercy and not sacrifice, you would not have condemned the guiltless," Samuel Sewall could see only one meaning. He had been wrong, dead wrong, culpably wrong, in seeing Satan in the guise of innocent citizens of Salem.

Therefore on the next Fast Day, January 14, 1697, three hundred years ago, Samuel Sewall, alone of all eight judges of the Salem trials, went to church, and as the minister walked to the pulpit at the beginning of the afternoon service, Sewall handed him a written confession and asked him to read it to the congregation.

Mr. Willard at some point in the service announced the confession, and Samuel Sewall stood up in his front pew during the reading, which went as follows:

> Samuel Sewall, sensible of reiterated strokes of God upon himself and family, and being sensible, that as to the Guilt contracted upon the opening of the late Commission . . . at Salem, is, upon many accounts, more concerned than any that he knows of, Desires to take the Blame and shame of it, Asking pardon of men, And especially desiring prayers that God, . . . would pardon that sin and all his other sins . . . (and) that He would powerfully defend him against all Temptations . . . for the future.

And then Mr. Sewall sat down.

The Psalmist says, "The sacrifices of God are a broken spirit, a broken and a contrite heart, O God, thou wilt not despise," and "The fear of the Lord is the beginning of wisdom."

If so, the picture of Judge Samuel Sewall standing in Second Church and setting himself beneath the judgment of God and his fellow worshippers should help us to see that we never stand so tall as when we stoop low enough to confess our sins. For this is not just a picture of judgment. It is a scene of mercy too, more mercy, sadly, than was shown to the nineteen victims of the trials in unhappy Salem.

WHAT LOVE IS

I'VE HEARD a good many definitions of love, but I boil most of them down to two. The first is "I like it and I want it." I just love chocolate, and sunsets, and vacations on the Maine coast, and Julia Roberts, and Beethoven.

The second is its opposite. "Love is what you do for someone else." You ask nothing for yourself. You ask only what you can do for others. This is the kind of love Jesus often spoke of and this is what Saint Paul describes in the thirteenth chapter of his first letter to the Corinthians.

Well, I have for you a third definition of love, one first made by Saint Ignatius Loyola, who founded the Jesuit order in 1450 A.D. Here it is: Love is the exchange of goods.

That's right, the exchange of goods! Doesn't sound very altruistic, does it? An exchange! Why, that's nothing more than a trade, a swap, a quid pro quo. It reminds me of a man whom I'll call Jack. He used to tell his wife, "You be nice to Jack and Jack will be nice to you." As you might guess, they're not married anymore. Yet Loyola calls love the "exchange of goods." Why? Here's my guess, and I'll explain it by telling you about the Sunday sexton at King's Chapel.

Some years past our Sunday sexton retired, and we needed a man to open the church, pick up after the Saturday weddings, put the hymnals and prayer books in order, answer the phone, greet early morning tourists, light the candles, ring the church bell, keep out tourists during the service, close up the church after services, and do many more things. Well, a man applied and we hired him, and he became a part of our life and perhaps we were a part of his.

He always had a smile, a friendly word, a cup of coffee, and some news for me when I arrived on Sunday morning. He greeted parishioners and visitors with equal warmth. He was great with kids. He was always on top of things, and he never missed a beat. Most of us couldn't imagine Sunday mornings at King's Chapel without Ed.

And he seemed to enjoy the people and the work. He loved being there. We seemed to be the perfect match of gifts and needs. And none of us could have made that happen. No one could have made the match ex nihilo. It happened. It was a gift.

When Loyola says that love is the exchange of goods, he refers not only to this lovely equation between gift and need, the love of each party for the other, but also to the good intent that enabled each to find the other and to give to each other fairly and freely.

Love is not just the decision of each party, but the disposition that makes this possible. Lovers feel this when they say, "We don't know how we found each other, but it's been wonderful. Sometimes we feel as if someone was looking out for us."

Love makes possible the exchange of goods. The more I think about this, the more sense it makes to me. None of us can ever be happy just getting what we want. We soon tire of it and want more or something else, and then we're tired of that, and pretty soon we're tired and bored all the time. On the other hand, none of us can be happy giving all the time. We burn out. We get tired, sullen, and dutiful. We need to be fed and rested, looked at, and stroked.

True love for most mortals (excepting saints) is a balance between giving and receiving, loving our neighbor and loving ourselves, the exchange of goods. Love, God's love, makes possible this balance and exchange.

I have a little faith in my own goodness. I have a little more faith in the goodness of others. But more and more I trust the goodness, which makes our goodness possible. To me that's realism. Thank you, Loyola, for reminding us of this, and thank you, Ed, for being our Sunday sexton, and thank *you* for giving me a chance to say these things to you. You too are part of the exchange of goods.

HOW REAL LOVE COMES

SHE SAT in the small living room of her second-floor apartment, knitting a white sweater. Her daughter sat across the room and said to her, "Mother, he hasn't been here for thirty years. He isn't going to come back now."

"Not for us—I never said he would," the mother said. "But for him he will. He couldn't miss the service."

"Oh, mother," said the daughter. "You're a dreamer."

He was now a famous television producer in Rome. He had grown up in this Sicilian village where, as a fatherless boy, he fell in love with movies and was befriended by the projectionist at the local theater. There in the projection booth he learned how to operate the camera, how to wind and splice films, and above all how to open himself to the great myths of films. When he became a young man, he left the village and went to Rome and made lots of money and never, so far, had come back.

The old projectionist had died, and his mother had left a message at her son's apartment in Rome. Now she was waiting for him to call back. The phone never rang. But the doorbell did.

"It's him," said the old lady who had just finished a row in her knitting.

"Mother!" said her daughter.

The old mother laid down her knitting and got up from her chair. She did not notice, or did not seem to care, that in one hand she still held a knitting needle with a thread of yarn attached. She walked across the room, the yarn pulling jerkily out of the rows that she had so neatly knitted. If you were there, you could have marked the mother's progress along the second-floor hall, down the wide circling stairs, along the first-floor hall, and to the door by the unraveling of the white thread that followed her.

And then when the yarn stopped moving, you might have looked out the window of her apartment and down into the garden and seen an old woman embracing a tall and now gray-haired man in a rumpled but stylish suit. She was right. He had come back.

If anybody ever asked me to define love after seeing *Cinema Paradiso*, I would say it was the unraveling of a half-knit white sweater and the little dance that the white yarn made as it played across the living room floor, along the hall, the stairs, and the garden walk. That thread in some way symbolized the bond that held together this old Sicilian woman and her successful son in Rome and witnessed their reunion.

Love comes only in specifics. A handshake, a kiss, a cup of cold water, a faded photograph, a withered rose, a gold star in the window, real blood spilling down the stake of a real cross, or a dancing thread of thin white yarn.

HE WENT ON DANCING

HE WAS STANDING at the edge of the crowd at coffee hour, a slim, gray-haired man in a dark-brown double-breasted suit, waiting until other members of the congregation had thanked me for the sermon and then moved on. When the last one left, he shyly introduced himself. I'll call him Jim. After heartfelt thanks, he said my sermon made him think about his wife.

She was Irish, he said, with a good heart and a good soul and a strong body, so strong, in fact, that she lived for fifteen years with a degenerative nerve disease. Despite her illness she took the burden in raising their three children while Jim brought home the paycheck.

Two years before she died, he took an early retirement and stayed home to care for her. When he could no longer help her to the bathroom, he bathed and clothed her in bed, and all the time, he said, she never lost her good cheer.

"What was it like—after she died?" I asked.

Jim began to cry. Then he paused and said, "She gave me the greatest gift, a spiritual gift. She gave me courage.

Never, never did she complain. Before she died she said, 'Promise me one thing, that you will have joy.' "

"But after she died I went into a slump. I didn't want to do anything. I didn't want to go anywhere. I didn't want to live. I barely existed—until one morning, when I remembered what she had made me promise, that I would have joy. And then I felt her courage and," here Jim laughed "I started taking dancing lessons, and now I'm dancing in a local musical here."

I was struck by the power of this singular woman, but I was struck as well by the love in this singular man. You'll never read about Jim and his wife in the papers or see their faces on the television screen, but he is a hero and she is a heroine, and I want you to know that people like this have lived, still live.

This world is full of heroines and heroes, not just the famous ones, but the ordinary champions of the common daily struggle to survive, to make sense of life, and to help their neighbors, and I think it is my duty to tell their stories.

In a world that cannot understand the scriptures, these people are God's witnesses and remind us of our origins and destiny. They make God real. They are the saints.

MICHAEL DOHERTY,
AN ORDINARY BOY

HE WAS JUST an ordinary boy, born in Washington, D.C., to ordinary parents. He grew up near Sixteenth Street, in an area that was largely black. His parents moved to Boston, where he went to grade school and dropped out of high school after two years. He was quiet and didn't hang out with kids his age, but went to work to support his mother and disabled father. He did some fishing along the South Shore and wanted to become a fisherman, but he didn't have connections, so he settled for running a Goodwill store. Sometimes he lived with his aunt and sometimes with his parents.

He was planning to go back to school, but late on March 19, 1980, he was headed for his parents' house from Cambridge, waiting at the Columbia subway station, when we saw a disturbance at the far end of the platform. A gang of white youths was attacking a black man. Michael Doherty ran to help the man and succeeded in diverting the gang's anger toward himself. After trying to fight them off, he ran out of the station with the youths in pursuit. He ran across the Southeast Expressway, where an oncoming car hit and killed him instantly. His body was hurled between the guardrails where it wasn't found until two days later. The wake and the funeral were held at St. Peter's in Cambridge, and one of the things that people remarked about Michael Doherty was that he seemed such an ordinary boy.

I have wondered what went through Michael Doherty's mind when he saw the scuffling at the far end of the Columbia Station platform, and it has occurred to me that perhaps nothing went through his mind— certainly no platitudes about brotherhood. Perhaps something went, not through his mind, but through his heart. Someone was in trouble. Someone needed help. First he was willing to see, to notice. Then he followed the simple human instinct to reach out to help. He didn't know it would cost his life. He didn't have time to weigh the danger. If he had lived, he might have said that he was only doing what anyone would do. An ordinary thing. Perhaps it is the ordinary people attempting what they think are ordinary things who accomplish the most for their brothers and sisters.

The simple son of an Italian merchant established the Franciscan Order. A nondescript and bookish Belgian ministers to the lepers of Molokai. A young Yugoslavian peasant woman cares for the dying in Calcutta. A Galilean peasant became a prophet and God's symbol on this earth.

Perhaps the saints are ordinary people who would say that they were only doing what was expected of them, what anyone would do if one could see. Is that the key? Do the saints see where we only glance? Maybe the Levite and priest on the way to Jericho just saw a form beside the road. Only the Samaritan saw a man.

You and I have the power to see and reach out, the power to leave our isolation, the power to forget ourselves and be with another. May God give us the power to be an ordinary person like Michael Doherty.

THE DEATH OF ROMERO

ON MARCH 24, 1980, at 6:30 in the evening, the Archbishop of El Salvador, Oscar Arnulfo Romero, was saying mass in the small Chapel of Divine Providence attached to a diocesan hospital. He had just finished reading the Words of the Institution: "This is my body, which will be given for you; this is my blood, which is shed for you." At that point, a man waiting in the back of the church pulled out a gun, shot Romero in the head, and fled the church. Romero died moments later.

Earlier that day an American visitor had asked Romero if he shouldn't be more careful of his person, and Romero asked in reply how he could allow himself to be protected when his people were dying all around him.

The slaughter continued after Romero's death, in part because our government, yours and mine, to which we pay taxes, continued to support and finance forces in El Salvador that were guilty of torture, murder, and intimidation.

When a friend of mine returned from a two-week visit in El Salvador, he told me that it's hard for us to imagine what life in that country was like. In the eyes of the military and the right-wing paramilitary death squads, every refugee was suspect and anyone who helped the refugees was suspect. Being suspect meant that one could be summarily taken away, tortured, and killed.

In November of 1984, a Lutheran pastor, David Ernesto Espino, thirty-seven years old, married with children, was found shot in the head, his body hacked to pieces with a machete. Espino's crime was that he was working in the refugee camps, distributing food, arranging for medical advice, teaching, praying, distributing communion. Said an American Lutheran official, "The church lives in constant terror here, and anyone who works with refugees is seen as suspect by the right."

So the crucifixion continues. The only difference is that some people, Christians in particular, have a hope that God will vindicate their sufferings and by some miracle bring peace and order out of this butchery. Archbishop Romero himself voiced this hope when he said, "I have to confess that, as a Christian, I don't believe in death without resurrection. If they kill me, I will rise again in the Salvadoran people. I'm not boasting or saying this out of pride. Martyrdom is a grace of God that I don't feel worthy of. But if God accepts the sacrifice of my life, I hope that my blood will be like a seed of liberty and a sign that our hopes will soon become a reality."

When Romero died, there was a crucifix hanging in the Chapel of Divine Providence where he was celebrating mass. It was a conventional crucifix, a carved and painted figure of Christ with a crown of thorns, dying on a Roman cross. But at some point after Romero died, that crucifix was taken down. In its place the sisters in that hospital put up a cross, and at the intersection of the crossbar and the vertical, they set in a frame of golden rays flaming out from the center, where we usually see the figure of Christ, a mirror. The effect is startling. You look into the cross and in the place of Christ you see yourself.

If you are one who feels part of the Salvadoran people and part of their struggle to live in minimal justice and order, then you know that you are part of their crucifixion and that you may be part of their resurrection as well. You see that you are part of Christ in El Salvador and therefore Christ's work is your work, the work he announced to his startled listeners in the Nazareth synagogue:

> The spirit of the Lord God is upon me because he has anointed me to preach good news to the poor, to proclaim release to the captive and the recovering of sight to the blind, to set at liberty those who are oppressed, to proclaim the year of the Lord's favor.

Christ's words and ministry lived again in El Salvador in the sacrifice of Romero. Thanks be to God.

SO MANY LITTLE DEATHS

WHEN WE SAID goodbye to our son at Logan Airport, his sisters cried and his mother hugged him hard, and I did too, and he looked embarrassed. Then they announced his flight, and he walked down the long corridor to the plane. Every now and then he'd turn around to wave, and, yes, we were still there, and then he turned the corner and was gone.

It doesn't matter whether you leave by train or plane or car or on your own two feet, but there is always a corner that you must turn and then you're gone.

We walked back to the car parked on the top level of the garage, and, I imagine, we looked as if there'd been a death. In a sense, there had been, for every parting is a death, and so is every goodbye. We were giving up the someone we had heard bellowing in the shower at 5:00 in the morning, who ate the brownies his sister had baked for their friends, who left his bicycle in the front hall, who made quiet funny jokes and wonderfully crazy drawings, and who left emptiness and silence where he used to be.

So, yes, you must die to the one he was and die to the one you were to him, so that he and you can each go on and become the ones God created you to be, not the one you've grown comfortable with. This dying-to-each-other is as much a part of life as breathing and sleeping, but knowing that doesn't make it any easier.

So many little deaths we die before we die the big one. We die these deaths so we may live, so we may move with that inexorable force called life. The favorite mug smashed on the stone floor, the lost book, the job gone, the song sung, the face now seen only in that unrealistic photo—all these are part of the dying-to-live.

In the 1940s Dietrich Bonhoeffer sat in his prison cell in Berlin and wrote a letter to his parents. It was the first Christmas he had spent away from home and he wrote,

Nothing can fill the gap when we are away from those we love, and it would be wrong to try and find anything. We must simply hold out and win through. That sounds very hard at first, but at the same time it is a great consolation since leaving the gap unfilled preserves the bonds between us. It is nonsense to say that God fills the gap. He does not fill it but keeps it empty so that our communion with each other may be kept alive even at the cost of pain.

That's another way of making my point. Perhaps it is simply dying to the one thing or one person whom we love, so that, although we may not know it at the time, another thing, another person, another love, may happen—not take its place.

Three months after our son left, we returned to the airport to welcome him back. We knew that a young man would step off the plane at Logan Airport, and he would look very much like the one we said goodbye to. But he wouldn't be. He would be different, and we would be different too. That difference is good, and it would happen because we were willing to say goodbye, to die a bit so that we could grow a bit and meet each other as the people we became.

The church has known this for a long time and reminds us in the liturgies and scriptures. But every now and then we must rediscover it for ourselves. I guess Logan Airport is as good a place for that as any.

GRACE IN THE FACE OF PAIN

On an October afternoon in 1994 I walked to a hospital near my office to visit a woman who had been diagnosed with bone cancer. The cancer had spread to her spine and liver. She was taking painkillers and lay on a waterbed. She was good humored, gracious, clear about the threat that she faced, and she was in pain.

Around the same time I talked with a parishioner about a mutual friend and learned to my surprise about his abused and terrified childhood. If I read the account of his suffering in a book, I would hardly believe it. But it was true. My friend was in pain.

A high school classmate at a reunion not long before had told me of the man she loved, who would not or could not love her. And so she had said goodbye to him for probably the last time. She was in pain.

These three incidents remind me of the first truth of Buddhism: Life is painful, or Suffering is inevitably part of our existence.

In spite of all the songs and icons and stories that tell us how happy, prosperous, contented, and fulfilled we should be, we know the truth of our suffering. Aware of it or not, we must deal with our pain each day.

Often we look for a pill or a program or a person who will take away or ease the pain. And almost automatically we expect religion to reduce it, banish it, explain it, or transform it. In the 1930s, Bill Wilson and Dr. Bob Smith faced the pain that their drinking was causing them and others. And by the grace of God and with an incredible effort on their part, they turned their pain into good— for themselves and others.

So when we pray—whatever else we pray for or about—we must pray for the power to accept our pain and transmute it into something good.

I remember the water-meter reader who came to our house when we lived on Beacon Street. He walked with a bend in his back, and I asked him if his back was hurting. "Hurting!" he said. "It's killing me, but you know I give it up. I give it to God. Maybe it'll make somebody else a little better off."

Superstitious piety? I think not. Jesus came with the word and the gift of healing. In his name the church continues his ministry and offers the gift of healing through prayer, conversation, worship, and for centuries, through hospitals and hospices established all over the world. My father and mother were ministers of Christian healing in China; they were doctor and nurse.

Religious healing sometimes mends the body, sometimes the soul, sometimes both. Behind this ministry of healing lies human compassion and behind compassion lies God's will that we be whole. We need to seek healing when we are hurting. We need to go out and find the healer. We need to receive what the healer can do for us. And then we must accept the outcome, live with it, and learn from it.

The world is not without compassion. The world is not without healing. Through human hearts and human hands, God still brings mercy and release. The gift is there. It's ours for the asking.

DRUMS TELL THE STORY

CHRISTIANS CELEBRATE Good Friday in many ways: with fasting and hot cross buns, praying and teaching, stripping the altar, processing the cross, with the mass of the presanctified gifts, and preaching from noon to three o'clock. (That preaching service began in Lima, Peru, in 1787.)

Each year at King's Chapel on Good Friday evening, we read the story of the crucifixion as the church is slowly darkened. The service ends as the Christ candle is carried out of the sanctuary and the Bible is slammed shut.

But only in Spain, as far as I know, do they celebrate Good Friday with drums. Here is Luis Bunuel's account of Good Friday in his home village of Calanda. It's a long passage but well worth sharing:

> Back in my childhood only a couple hundred drummers were involved in this rite, but nowadays there are over a thousand, including six hundred to seven hundred drums and 400 bongos.

Toward noon on Good Friday the drummers gather in the main square opposite the church and wait there in total silence. When the first bell in the tower begins to toll, a burst of sound, like a terrific thunderclap, electrifies the whole village, for all the drums explode at the same instant. A sort of wild drunkenness surges through the players; they beat for two hours until the procession forms, then leave the square and make a complete tour of the town.

During the procession everyone chants the biblical story of the Passion. By five o'clock the ceremony is over, and there is a moment of silence, until the drums begin again, to continue until noon on the following day. By the early hours of Saturday the skin on the drums is stained with blood, even though the beating hands belong to work-worn peasants.

On Saturday many villagers put down their drums and retrace Calvary, climbing the Way of the Cross on a hillside near the village. The rest continue beating, however, until everyone gathers at seven o'clock for the funeral procession. As the bell tolls the noon hour on Saturday, the drums fall silent, but even after the normal rhythms of life have been re-established, some villagers still speak in an oddly halting manner, an involuntary echo of the drums of Good Friday.

I can barely imagine what that might be like, but the wordless drums, it seems to me, could speak as clearly as any voice on Good Friday. A hundred or a thousand drums can tell the story of triumph and tragedy as well as any words. The bloodstained hands of Spanish peasants bear witness to the faith as fittingly as the strained vocal chords of the local priest.

God's varied voices astound us. God speaks even through drums.

THE SOULS OF OUR CHILDREN

QUAKER EDUCATOR Parker Palmer describes a new principal, a Filipino émigré who had just arrived at a troubled inner-city school in Dayton, Ohio. This school had been plagued with fights, truancy, abysmally low academic records, and a pervasive sense of despondency among its demoralized teachers.

The first thing this new principal did was to call the faculty together, and he said to his disheartened colleagues,

> We have to understand that the young people at our school have nothing of external substance or support. They come from dangerous neighborhoods. They have poor places to live, little food, parents who themselves are on the ropes and therefore unable to pay attention to them.

> But these students have one thing that no one can take away from them. They have their souls. And from this day on, we are going to lift up those souls. We are going to make those souls visible to the young people themselves, to their parents, and

to this community. We are going to celebrate those souls, and we are going to reground their lives in the power of their souls.

And this will require that we, the faculty, recover the power of our own souls, remembering that we too are soul-driven, soul-animated creatures.

Parker Palmer added that this was the beginning of a dramatic turnaround for that school.

I was stunned by these words from an unknown, unnamed, and in some ways alien principal. Everything he said stands against a culture that devastates us with words, music, icons, images, scenes, and choices that would, if we yielded, reduce us to the status of nothing more than mere voters, consumers, workers, commuters, viewers, and listeners—beings without souls, without a shred of transcendent reference.

Beginning with the simple radical assumption that we are above all soul-driven beings, a Midwestern principal changed a community that had lost its identity and hope for the future.

And then I heard a mother in my church describe her role as a mother. She said, "I believe that my most important job is to protect the souls of my children." Did you hear that? The *souls* of her children.

Other parents worry about their children's grades, health, performance at Little League games, their keyboard and computer skills, their music lessons, their summer camps, in short, everything that points to getting ahead in the world. You know as well as I do that a child can become a perfect performer in this world, can succeed in school, sports, and the marketplace, and at the same time become either a rotten person or a miserable professional.

Jesus asked, "What does it profit a man (or a woman) if they gain the whole world and lose their own soul?" A person with no sense of his or her own soul must either be feared or pitied.

This mother in my church thinks it is soul above all else that makes a child or man or woman a human being. This is the world we live in. Affairs are now soul-size. It has always been true. Maybe we will learn it again.

EVERY SAINT HAS A PAST

WE HAD A GOOD laugh when we saw the front page of
The Boston Globe and read the article about Michael
Dongarra, a guest for seven months at Glastonbury
Abbey in Hingham, and featured not long before on
the television program *America's Most Wanted*. He had
previously visited several other religious communities
and stolen crosses, candlesticks, statues, vestments, two
fifteenth-century religious paintings, Russian Orthodox
icons, several pews, and an entire altar from Notre Dame
convent in San Francisco. He had also practiced as an
unlicensed psychologist in Massachusetts and been dis-
barred after filing claims for more than seventy thousand
dollars in bogus fees.

Michael Dongarra arrived at Glastonbury Abbey in
April of 1996 and worked as groundskeeper while
beginning what he said was his novitiate among the
twelve monks who comprise that community. Abbot
Nicholas Morcone, who must be grateful that the abbey
lost nothing during Dongarra's stay, said, "If he was
hoping to hide out, this would be a good place. We are

hardly a high-profile bunch of people." Michael Dongarra went to the right place. Refuge is an old tradition in the Christian church, inherited from Jewish and Roman practice. A fugitive from justice could run to a temple, church, or monastery, and once within its precincts be safe from mob or the police, at least for a time.

In England, for example, the fugitive on reaching the church or abbey had to surrender his arms, confess his sin to a priest, swear to obey the rules of the house, pay an admission fee, and wear a black gown with Saint Cuthbert's cross embroidered on the left shoulder. If he behaved himself for forty days, he might then make restitution of his theft and safely leave the country.

Churches and abbeys that provided such havens were called sanctuaries. Maybe we're not so different from Michael Dongarra. He may or may not have been a penitent when he came to Glastonbury, but he needed to escape, and so do we.

All of us who seek an abbey, a cathedral, or a church are seeking sanctuary from one sin or another. We're all fugitives—some of us from work, some of us from relationships gone rotten, some of us from ourselves. And some of us, like Michael Dongarra, from justice.

We are fugitives from passions, obsessions, addictions, miscalculations, bad decisions, and all the other dangerous clutter that we have carried for far too long. We need to retreat. None of us can survive without a retreat.

Sleeping is a retreat. Television, reading, gardening, playing bridge, walking, tennis, bowling, Lord, even golf, are retreats from the madness of getting too much or not getting enough. Even if we're not escaping from the law, we are often like Jonah still trying to escape from God.

The good news is that we cannot escape the hound of heaven. Like Michael Dongarra, we must confront God's judgment and all our sins, but like him we may meet God's mercy too and in that mercy find his promise. Every saint has a past and every sinner has a future. That's good news.

EVEN IN GALILEE

JOHN'S GOSPEL describes how the people who have just heard Jesus preaching begin to argue about whether he is a troublemaker or the Messiah. At one point Nicodemus (that's right, the one who went to see him under the cover of night) defends Jesus, and his critics ask Nicodemus, "Are you from Galilee too? Read the scriptures and you will see that no prophet ever came from Galilee."

What was it about Galilee that made these people suspicious? They seemed to think that nobody important would ever come from there. Why? Galilee was the last corner of Palestine to be converted to Judaism and subdued by the Romans. A tough, raw mountain people whose rustic accent stood out like a sore thumb on the streets of Jericho and Jerusalem, the Galileans were enforced and therefore unreliable converts.

Galilee was not just Hicksville to acculturated Jews. It was rebel territory, more likely to produce a mutiny than a Messiah. We would be as likely to expect a political reformer to come from a squad of the Michigan militia as they would be to expect a Messiah from Galilee.

But the Bible narrative is filled with turnarounds. Again and again in the New Testament and the Old, we read that God's emissary appears where we least expect it. Moses comes from the courts of Pharaoh, David from the village of Bethlehem, the brothers Maccabaeus from farm country, and Jesus from Galilee.

Jesus told his listeners time and again that it was pointless to look here or there for the Messiah. He warned them against false prophets and false Christs. Only God, not even the Son, knew when and where Israel's savior would appear. I translate this to mean that if we fixate on one image of Christ, however good—the Christ of the ghetto or the barrio, the Christ of the liberation seminar, the Christ of liturgical purity, the Christ of theological correctness, or the Christ of spirituality—if we fixate on any single image of where and in whom God might appear, we can only be sure that we will miss the Messiah. This is the sin of premature specificity.

Dame Julian of Norwich warns her readers not to look too hard for God in the specifics, but to keep a strong and general expectation, trusting God to be known to us when we are ready.

That makes sense to me. We must wait and hope, and if our waiting seems like madness to a world bent on suicide, nonetheless that hope, that waiting for the word to make itself manifest, is all we need to keep going.

Hope is not a luxury. Hope is not a virtue. Hope is essential for those who wish to live with strength, gratitude, and good cheer in a failing world.

God's word and God's emissary will appear when we most need them—from anywhere—Michigan, Boston, and perhaps even Galilee.

YOUR FEET WILL TAKE YOU

YOUR FEET WILL TAKE YOU

YOU CAN PRAY in many ways—by reading aloud in church, by meditating alone, by chanting, contemplative reading, fasting, staring through an icon, dancing, and—you can pray by walking! Walking is one of the oldest ways to pray in the world, but not every kind of walking is prayerful. The walking must be purposeful, focused on God or on the way to God. For example, monks in Christian monasteries often walk in the garden with their breviaries and pray as they walk. When Chartres Cathedral was built in about 1200, the architects laid a pattern of tesserae into the stone floor, giving the pilgrims a pattern to follow as they walked and prayed.

Pilgrims walk the path of Jesus, the Via Dolorosa, to the Shrine of the Holy Sepulchre in Jerusalem. In England pilgrims walk from their homes to Whitby, Walsingham, and Canterbury. European pilgrims walk to Chartres, Maria Laach, and Saint James Compostela. Mexican peasants walk to the shrine of Our Lady of Guadalupe. As one who walks the streets of Boston and hills of New Hampshire, I have learned something. If you want to know a place—a city, a country, a neighbor-hood—walk it. The slower you walk, the more you will see. The more you see, the more you will enjoy it. The more you enjoy it, the more you will love it. The more you love it, the more it will be yours. Your feet will take you on the way of the heart.

I am heartened by the efforts of people like Alan French, Gordon Shaw, Peter Forbes, and Nancy Merrill who have succeeded in creating a two-hundred-mile footpath that will circle metropolitan Boston. Beginning in Duxbury, the Bay Circuit Trail circles west, north, and eastward through forty-eight towns that lie between Routes 128 and 495, and ends at the Joppa Flats Sanctuary on Plum Island.

Why am I so heartened by this? Because I believe that if we walk the land, we will love the land and learn to be loyal to it. Fly over it, and you don't know it's there. Drive by it, you scarcely care. Walk it? You are part of it.

I like to think that in the years to come our children will be walking through the woods, towns, and fields of this country on trails that we built or planned or dreamed of. I like to think that those who walk will become pilgrims on the path to our survival. I like to think that our walking and theirs will become a prayer for our future. Surely, this too is the work of God.

A BLIZZARD, A BLESSING,
AND A SERVICE

BEFORE I EVEN walked into the office on that snowy, blowy, and blindingly cold Wednesday in January, Marco had already called to say that, yes, he would play the organ for the midday service, and Carol Genovese called from Brookline to say that she would read the lesson. And as I walked over the Hill in front of the State House, I could hear the King's Chapel bell calling people to prayer, so I knew that Christine had opened up the church. When I walked through the door, the lights were on, the candles were lit, and the place was warm despite the storm outside.

We had eight people in church in the middle of a blizzard: Joe and his wife from Somerville, Bill from Beacon Hill, Carol from her office in Copley Square, Mary Jane and Jonathan, and, oh dear, someone I can't recall from nearby. We read the noonday prayers, and I preached, and we sang "O God our help" and listened to Marco's magnificent postlude, and then we all sat down to tea, bread, cheese, and a jolly conversation.

If some dour skeptic had asked us why we were there, why we had tramped through the snow for a half-hour service, why we hadn't stayed in our nice warm homes and offices, why we hadn't canceled church, we probably would have laughed and given an inadequate answer but known from the glow in our hearts that we were right in being there, especially on that vastly inconvenient day.

I once heard an orthodox Jew describing all he and his wife went through in order to maintain a kosher kitchen, and someone asked him, "Why do you go through all that? It's so inconvenient." And the orthodox Jew answered him, "I do it *because* it's inconvenient."

That's not even half an answer, but it's what you say to someone who lives his life in terms of comfort, convenience, and ease. What you don't say is the blessing you receive, the sense of balance, the clarity and charity that come to you through wonderfully inconvenient customs such as praising God at 3:00 in the morning every day of the year or at noon in the midst of a blizzard.

Behind the inconvenience stands the blessing, and only those who believe in the blessing, who have tasted the goodness of the Lord, who are tired of comfort and convenience, will assume the tasks and disciplines of daily prayer and weekly worship and reading tales of conversion. The good news is that those disciplines and their rewards are always there.

HUNGRY FOR LIFE WITH GOD

IN THE LAST YEAR I've been reading books by and
about monks and nuns, men and women who have left
city hall, the college, the hospital, the law office, the lab,
and the church, left their apartments and friends and
clubs and sandlot softball teams and gone to live with
other refugees from civilization, sometimes in a desert,
sometimes on a mountain, sometimes in a suburb, sometimes even in a city.

These men and women moved to abbeys in part
because they felt uneasy with the way they lived in main-
stream society. But they moved in part because they hun-
gered for life with God in community with others. The
representative of these men and women whom we know
best in this country is probably Thomas Merton. New
books of his appear each year; old ones are republished
regularly. The monks and nuns I've met were no such dis-
tinguished writers. Most of them left no literary legacy.
Many left only a few sentences and two or three reported
conversations. A few wrote a great deal. I read their words
early in the morning before I read the newspapers.

After studying the words from these monks and nuns, the daily newspapers, with their dull and daily retelling of the ancient themes of greed, fear, cruelty, violence, conflict, and occasionally some touching tale of kindness or wisdom, seem curiously unimportant. I have come to doubt that the answer to the world's problems will come from academics, senators, presidents, bureaucrats, lecturers, and workshop leaders. I have come to believe that what we must know in order to survive as humankind will be found in abbeys, monasteries, and hermitages. René Descartes said that all the ills of humankind come from our inability to sit quietly in a room alone for one hour. Now that's simplistic, isn't it?

Look at the immense problems of global warming, economic injustice, oppressed minorities of race and clan and gender, ethnic rivalries, overpopulation, vanishing forests and ozone layer, rising tides and temperatures— I could go on and on. And you could say with some assurance that no simple solution can be found.

Why do I say that abbeys are the keys to our survival? Because they have much to teach us. People who live in these abbeys must practice three things: solitude, simplicity, and community.

Solitude: a life with God.
Simplicity: a life with few things.
Community: a life with people.

In all three cases one must devote one's life to *not* being the center of the universe. In solitude, we let God direct our lives. In simplicity, we use only what we need. Through compassion, we give ourselves to others.

No monk, no nun, no human being can reach perfection, but we can try to live this kind of life. The intention, not the accomplishment, makes this life a saving life. Dour as it may sound to us, that life has brought deep happiness to millions of people around the world through countless centuries.

I speak as one to whom this monastic life makes more and more sense. I do not intend to join a monastery. I do not intend to move to a mountain, wilderness, or desert. My question is: How does one live this life in the city, in society, in the midst of the madness of civilization? How can we live these values in the midst of the world? I doubt that God calls us all to abbeys, but I believe that God calls us all to solitude, simplicity, and community.

It's strange to think that the abbeys might save world, but we have trusted stranger thoughts than this.

A CHURCH INSIDE GATWICK

SOME PLACES seem real to me: kitchens, vegetable gardens, town dumps, mountain trails, churches. Some places seem unreal to me: shopping malls, Copley Place, Disneyland, and, above all, airports.

Airports are not places where you live. They are places you go through, and the faster, the better. They are clean, comfortable, efficient, expensive, and non-human. I find Logan a bit more tolerable than others. After all, it's close to home. But LaGuardia, Gatwick, Heathrow, Hartwell, Orly, and O'Hare are something else.

I went through Gatwick this summer on my way home from visiting my sister. I was leaving on a weekend, and when I entered Gatwick, I saw the place jammed with charter groups: Crowd City. People were tired, anxious, resentful, as I was, at having to return. Lines were long and tempers short. Gatwick was not lovely.

The airport personnel were courteous. They did their best to move the lines quickly, but there were so many people, and each passenger required attention with his or her luggage, security, passports, last-minute shopping, and, for some, flight changes. I had almost reached the luggage counter when an announcement came over the PA system: "Holy Communion will be celebrated in the airport chapel at 10:30 this morning. Members of the free churches are welcome to attend."

Holy Communion? But of course. It was Sunday. But in an airport? Can you imagine hearing that announcement at Logan? As soon as I'd checked my bags, I went looking for the chapel and found it behind a plastic door in a plastic wall. Once I opened the door, I saw a lovely room—square, with a soft green carpet the color of heather and about twenty-five comfortable chairs arranged in two semicircles around a simple altar with a white cloth and unlit candles. There were three people in the chapel when I entered, but within two minutes of my arrival, they left. "Oh great," I thought. "It's going to be me and the priest. Same old story. As soon as things get serious, everybody leaves the church."

I stayed, and the priest, a surprisingly young man, came in, nodded to me, lit the candles, arranged a couple of books, and went out. Then a middle-aged lady came in and sat down. Then a young man. Then a dark-skinned couple—(from India, perhaps), and others, and others. By the time the priest returned in his vestments, the chairs were full, and a few people were standing in the back of the room.

And so we had communion that morning, a simple half-hour service with a brief homily and prayers for the world, for peace in the Mideast, for the people who worked at the airport (strange, I hadn't thought of them), and for everyone who was traveling that day. What a circle of love you can create with the right intention and a few good words.

We passed the peace to each other (that is, we shook hands and said "Peace" or "God's peace be with you"), and we were strangers no more. I don't recall where I have felt such spontaneous and natural warmth at any service. It seemed to me that our common danger and this common promise brought us together.

Then we went forward to the bread and wine, and after a brief prayer and benediction, it was over. But here's what surprised me: The people stayed in their chairs and chatted with each other! It was amazing. As we left, the young priest asked each of us our destination and asked God's blessing on our journeys.

That's what a good liturgy can do. It can transform our perception of a place or a person. What may seem on first sight common, dull, or even unpleasant becomes real. The liturgy does this by bringing the people and place into the presence of God. For a moment or an hour we see that place and people as God sees them.

I see airports differently now. They are not impersonal but filled with people, real people: workers, travelers, families saying hello or good-bye, children, women, and men for whom Christ lived and died. Gatwick will never be the same for me, not Logan, nor Heathrow, nor even O'Hare. Even airports are part of creation. And God is there.

BEHIND THE PULPIT

FROM TIME to time during my tenure as minister at King's Chapel, I would preach in other churches, and when I did, I always looked to see what I would find behind the pulpit. From the pews the pulpit is a paneled facade, but behind that facade your pastor, rector, priest, or rabbi conceals those things he or she thinks necessary to survive a Sunday morning or a Friday evening.

One finds the predictable box of throat lozenges, the bottle of Pertussin, Fisherman's Friend, aspirin, Tylenol, or Pepto-Bismol. There is the glass of water from the last service, the box of Kleenex, a hymnal, pencils, ballpoint pens, chalk, a beat-up Bible, masking tape, and sometimes last Sunday's sermon. There may be burnt-out candles, battered sheet music, a faded stole, matchbooks, lighters, and Sterno cans, an amplifier for the PA system, at times a stool on which short preachers stand in order to be seen, sometimes a toy or prop from a children's story.

On my first pulpit exchange, I found this note behind the pulpit: "Remember professional ethics. Don't try to be too good." Now that was a compliment. I've never found a bottle of sherry, a scarf, or a clip-on bow tie.

Look behind the pulpit, and you'll see the preacher as a human being. You'll see the preacher's fear of losing her voice, losing his way, losing her mind. The one who stands before you in that great black robe with swelling shoulders on a Sunday morning, the one who stands above you and speaks for God—at least as far as your church lets anyone speak for God—lives in constant, if suppressed, anxiety about how things will go at 11:00 on Sunday morning.

Preachers can rarely worship with you because they must constantly be thinking of what comes next and how it will come off. That's their job, and so they need their little arsenal of pick-me-ups: pills, lozenges, syrups, a little cache of pens and pencils, cards, Bibles, matches, lighters, what have you.

I have a suggestion. Why not surprise your pastor? Why not some Sunday morning leave a plate of cookies on the shelf behind the pulpit, or a sweet roll, raisin bran muffin, or perhaps just a jigger of single malt? Leave a love note anonymously or a wish-you-well card, and see the expression on her face, his face, when she or he comes up into the chancel.

You know it's pretty lonely up there, especially when you work so hard greeting people and thinking about them and worrying about them. A national Be-Kind to Preachers Week? We could institute this as an alternative to burn-out Sunday. Well, that's enough. Oh, you're wondering what you would find behind the pulpit of King's Chapel? Not much, we haven't room, but once in a while I found a single flower, and when I did, it warmed my heart because I knew the lady who had left it there. We've lived together for more than forty years.

TRUST THE WRITER

NOT LONG AGO I listened to a storyteller, a psychiatrist named Allen Chinen. He tells fairy stories about elderly people, and then leads discussions of these stories.

At the beginning of his talk Chinen said, "Of course, in order to enjoy and understand a fairy story, you must suspend belief, unlike what you do when you hear the Bible and are expected to believe."

Well, it occurred to me that you can't understand the Bible unless you are willing to suspend belief. Folks who don't get the Bible are often the same people will not give up for even a short time their belief in a Newtonian universe, or a creationist universe, or a historical universe where truth is strictly linear. Like Jack Webb on *Dragnet* they want "just the facts, ma'am." Could a whale have swallowed Jonah? Until we settle that question, we go no farther. Could a boy have killed a giant with a slingshot? How could bread be multiplied upon the hillside? Was the man really blind before Jesus healed him? The fundamentalists say "Yes," skeptics say "No," liberals say "Maybe," and none of them gets the point.

We can't get what the Bible says until we open our minds at all levels to what God is saying through the text. When we respond with *all* our faculties—intellect, memory, and imagination—and let the play of words and metaphors move through our minds and bring us wisdom, we may "get it."

But first we must suspend belief. That means that we must be willing to trust the scriptures, at least while we are reading them. We trust some truth to come from our encounter with the text. We may be hearing it in church, reading it at home, studying it in class, or pondering it on a retreat. And what happens? Hearing or reading scripture gives clarity and centeredness to the world we live in. Again and again I meet men and women who read the Bible with faith and intelligence and find meaning for their lives without giving away their brains or conscience. That's how scripture works.

When I think of the Jesus Seminar, that gang of two-to-three-hundred scholars who are knocking their brains out trying to decide which sayings of Jesus (and now Saint Paul!) are truly his, probably his, maybe his, not his, and print the words upon the page in varying shades of red, pink, gray, and black so that the reader will not be duped—and these scholars believe that they can do this—I am absolutely flabbergasted by their effort.

Whether I am reading poems by Robert Frost, plays by Shakespeare, quantum physics, or the Bible, I begin by trusting the writer. I will have questions in time, and plenty of them, but in order to learn, first I suspend belief.

THE LEAST OF MY BROTHERS

I saw him as soon as I went into the reading desk. The sexton had warned me that a strange young man had visited the church a few times, and today he'd come again and asked if he could attend the noontime service.

The sexton seated him way down front, several pews away from the rest of the congregation. When we stood for the first hymn, this man stood up as well, but bobbing and weaving as if he had Parkinson's or epilepsy. We read the psalm and everyone sat down. He didn't. He stood there in his pew while I read the service, weaving and bobbing, and then suddenly sat down and didn't get up for the rest of the service. He was slumped in his pew so low I thought he'd died or gone to sleep.

At the end of the service, I greeted people in the back and then walked down the side aisle to the Vestry where the luncheon crowd was already talking up a storm. I cast a quick glance at the stranger. He was still slumped in the pew.

Most of us were through lunch and conversation when suddenly he appeared in the doorway. A closer look at him showed a scraggly beard, a bent figure, eyes with an uncertain focus, a dark blue baseball cap, and clothes from the barrel.

Someone stood up and offered him a seat, and he took it without a word. Another pushed a plate of sandwiches toward him, and Eleanor asked him if he'd like tea or coffee. "Coffee," he said. And then the smell hit us—overpowering. Clearly the man was incontinent. The next twenty-five minutes were difficult for those who stayed, but several did and treated the stranger with polite and sometimes sad attention. They braved the stench, watched his jerky attempts to eat, and listened to his mumbling explanations (hit by a car three years ago). They wiped up the coffee when he spilled it and poured him a second cup. And one of them gave him his coat, for it was cold outside. At length, he left.

I was proud of our Wednesday noon gang. They had come through, and I thought of them several Sundays later when I read the familiar words from the twenty-fifth chapter of Matthew: "I was hungry and you gave me food, I was thirsty and you gave me drink, I was a stranger and you welcomed me. As you did it to the least of my brothers, you did it to me."

GOOD MEDICINE

IF SOMEONE you knew were suffering from chronic pain or a serious illness, what would you think if I told you that there is a procedure that has been tried for centuries and proven successful in reducing the pain and anxiety of many sick people, and in some cases of affecting cures? What would you think if I told you that this procedure would cost you nothing, but added that it had been at best ignored if not disparaged by most of the medical profession? What would you think if I told you that in a double-blind study performed on 393 patients at the San Francisco General Hospital and reported in the *Southern Medical Journal*, July 1988, this procedure had been shown by statistically significant proportions to help patients on the coronary care floor?

And then what would you think if I told you that this procedure was called prayer? You may feel incredulous and even irritated as I tell you this, and if you do, that's alright with me because I'm a skeptic on most things myself. Or you may be thinking, "So what's new? I've known that for years."

However you respond, might you agree that at least half of good health depends on the will to be healthy? The will to be healthy depends not just on our genes and history but on our state of mind as well.

People who feel abused, misused, or unused are going to have a harder time staying healthy than those who feel that despite the bad hands the world has dealt them, someone wishes them well, wants them well, wants them happy. That someone may be a spouse, a child, a colleague, a congregation, or a deity that cares for them. How many times people have told me that they got through tough times because, even alone and apparently abandoned, they felt this powerful sense of being loved, supported, encouraged. They felt that they had someone, or something, on their side.

Alexis Carrell, the famous English physician, visited the shrine at Lourdes at the turn of the twentieth century and witnessed a healing he could hardly believe. A young woman on the train to Lourdes was so sick that she seemed to be close to death. Carrell checked her vital signs on the train and again as she was being carried to the shrine. And then he saw her at that shrine transformed from a dying person into a living person. He saw a healing and reported it in a little book he wrote.

What impressed Carrell just as much as this healing was the peace and painlessness he saw in dying patients. Their presence at the shrine spoke of a world of spirit that he'd never seen in London hospitals. I myself have seen prayer not only cure people but also prepare them for death and help the friends and family around them through their dying. That too can be a powerful gift, to come out of another's dying with a sense of faith and courage.

Yes, even the daughter who sat for a couple of hours at the bedside of her dead mother and talked to her, and prayed with her, came out of that experience with a transforming and ennobling grief and gratitude. She wrote me about it later when she had returned to her life and work with a full heart.

"More things are wrought by prayer than this world dreams of." That's as true now as when Tennyson wrote those words a century ago. Healing is by no means the only reason for prayer, but prayer is good medicine for illness, tonic for the journey at any stage.

NEVER SIMPLY A CHURCH

THERE'S A STRANGE yarn told in the Gospel of John. John the Baptist and two of his own disciples are on a street in Bethany when Jesus walks by. John the Baptist says, "Look, here is the lamb of God." The two disciples leave John and walk after Jesus. Jesus turns around and says to them, "What do you want?" The men ask him, "Teacher, where are you staying?" Jesus says, "Come and see." They follow him to his inn—or perhaps it was a rooming house or a friend's spare room—and they talk until 4:00 in the morning.

Now that's the story, all of it, but of course a story in scripture is never just a story. There's always more. That's the mark of a classic. There's always more.

Jesus stayed somewhere in Bethany, and I wouldn't be surprised if today someone wasn't selling Popsicles, beads, and T-shirts in front of a house with a sign in front saying "Jesus Slept Here."

But could anything be less important to us? Places, sites, buildings, houses are the space, not the center, of religion. The house of Christ is never simply a church, cathedral, meetinghouse, or chapel. That may be the *place* of the encounter, but it is not *the* encounter.

The house of Christ is the community, a network of encounters. He told his disciples that they would be his sanctuary. His joy would be in them, his peace in them, his life with God in them and their successors, meaning us.

Christ is in the gathering of his people, wherever they gather—around a kitchen table, around a sick bed, around an open Bible, in a soup kitchen, in a demonstration, or in a lecture room hearing an exposition of faith. Christ's house is the people of God.

Remember when David said to God, "I've built myself a palace and now I'm going to build you a house, a really splendid temple." And remember God said to David, "You're going to build me a house? No, *I'm* going to build *you* a house, a lineage, a people who will carry on your kingdom."

The community that we enjoy is not something we made. It's a gift, all those wonderful, crazy, splendid people who sing in our choirs and sit in our pews and pray for us and behave sometimes like idiots and sometimes like saints, like us. Like us, they are the house of Christ, and we are privileged to dwell there, and to know Christ through them.

IN THE WORLD
BUT NOT PART OF IT

———————————

THREE FRIENDS of mine, Bruce, Tom, and George, share a singular life. They are monks; they live with fifty other monks in a cluster of stone buildings on the top of a hill west of Worcester. They spend most of their days in silence, broken by seven sung services and such conversation as is needed to run the community and produce a prodigious amount of jams and jellies, the abbey fund-raiser.

If you asked them why they chose this life, why they spend four to five hours a day chanting psalms and prayers, praying alone, and living under a strict rule, they'd probably tell you that they felt called to this for the sake of their own salvation. But if you pressed them further and asked them what they do for the world beside produce jams and jellies, they would probably tell you that they pray. They pray for others.

If there was a day when most people considered this a good way to spend one's time, that day is gone. Praying? All day? Don't they do anything else? Well, of course, they do. They cook, clean, wash clothes, maintain the buildings, care for their sick, make jams and jellies. But the main purpose of these men, and their colleagues in abbeys around the world, male and female, is prayer.

My mother, a missionary nurse, once visited a Buddhist abbey at the top of a mountain near the hospital where she worked in China. When she returned, she wrote a poem that ended,

> In the world but not part of it,
> I thought as we turned to go.
> We must carry the peace of the mountaintop
> To the sick ones there below.

That probably says it for most Westerners.

I got a different angle on monasteries from an article by a man who rode the rails westward with two hoboes named Slim and Beargrease. After freezing in boxcars for sixteen hours, he'd had enough and flew home. He left his companions with a sense of respect, and as he flew over the mountains where they were still riding the cars, he thought of them as two men who were enjoying the freedom that many office-bound, suburban captives would love to have.

He wrote, "They made me think of those alpine cloisters where penitents renounce the world only to spend their lives praying for it. Prayer takes many forms: kneeling, walking, maybe even riding the rails. Yet, how odd when you think of it, that strangers should pray for us.

Or for that matter, that grandiose characters like Slim and Beargrease might somehow fancy themselves as being free for us."

Suddenly, these lines made it clear for me. Like most Westerners I saw humanity as walking separate paths, which sometimes intersected, but then continued on their ways alone and isolated. "Do your own praying. Do your own walking. Do your own living. Nobody else can do it for you."

But the monks and the hoboes believe that we are somehow connected, perhaps by a web of invisible interaction. What the hobo sees from the door of the boxcar and what the monk sees in his cell and at chapel, the beauty of the mountains and the peace of God, may somehow be communicated to you and me.

Lost in our chitchat, sitcoms, errands, commuting, budgets, phone calls, email, taxes, and taking out the trash, we are still touched by the quest of pilgrims and solitaries, who have chosen the quest for essence over survival or success. We are touched by the lives lived in solitude.

And this gave me a sense that the prayers I say for others and the prayers we say at King's Chapel on Sunday morning and Wednesday noon may touch others who do not know us—the folks in the coffee shop, in the office, on the beach, on the run. For we are all part of the same land. None of us is an island.

NO EXPLANATIONS IN CHURCH

I LOVE THE SIGNS I find in churches. Some warn, some instruct, some irritate, some remind, and some tell a story. For example, in a village church in England, I found this inscription:

In loving memory of Hugh Rose Pope
Born June 17th, 1889
He fell asleep on October 7th, 1912, while climbing alone in the Pyrenees on the Pic du Midi d'Oussau where he rested for nine days in God's most holy sight. There went out from England to search for him Geoffrey Winthrop, Claude A. Elliott, Arnold H.M. Young, Nigel C. Madan, E.N.A. Finlay, by whose hands he was lowered into his grave in his mother's presence on October 18, 1912.

Love is of God.

I could almost see that graveyard scene before me.

Some signs warn us. In Saint Andrew's church in Colney, England, I found this one:

Sacred to the memory of John Fox, who on the 20th of December, 1806, in the 79th year of his Age was unfortunately kill'd near this spot having been thrust down and trampled on by the Horses of a Waggon. Tho his life was humble yet it is deserving of imitation. He was a worthy and useful Member of Society, an honest and industrious laborer. READER If thou drivest a team, be careful and endanger not the Life of another or thine own.

That's good for now as well.

Some signs instruct. In Norwich Cathedral, I found these words by a South American theologian, Dom Helder Camara. It read, "I gave food to the poor and they called me a saint. I asked why the poor have no food and they called me a communist."

Some signs irritate us. Near the exit of one historic church I read this notice: "Now you may leave but not before leaving us a contribution." I left that church not a penny lighter and guiltless as well.

Some signs remind us gracefully of what we owe to others. At the foot of a World War I memorial I read these simple words: "They gave their tomorrows for our today." Not bad.

My favorite sign was on the door of the Franciscan church in Nazareth. The intent of its author was to tell tour leaders to be silent when they and their charges were in the sanctuary. But the message didn't quite come through. The sign read: "No Explanations in Church."

It may not have worked in silencing the tourists, but it sure worked for me. That sign should be nailed to the lectern of every pulpit in America. I've heard great stories and great texts and great thoughts ruined by some damn-fool explanation that killed whatever beauty, truth, or wisdom was in the original. No explanations in church. You bet.

A great church, of course, needs no explanations, be it large or small. A great church tells its own story without our words and thoughts. It needs only our footsteps, and our attention.

Malcolm Miller, the resident English guide at Chartres Cathedral, said, "This church is a library written in stone and glass. There are many books here by many authors, but they all point to one theme. You can learn that theme from reading any part, but first you must learn to read."

The signs in a church are part of the testimony of the whole structure, and the building itself is a testimony to the faith of all the folk who worshipped there throughout its life.

Thanks be to God.

THE ULTIMATE INTIMACY

THE SUBJECT assigned for our discussion was intimacy, and I was a tad nervous. I tend to keep a decent distance from my peers. I watch the psychic space around me. I hate the enforced and phony disclosures that some therapy group leaders try to elicit from their victims. But I also prize true intimacy, those delicious moments, unrehearsed, unexpected, unmanageable, fragile, and unforgettable.

As the members of my group began to discuss the topic, I began to see how subtle and sweet was our common experience of intimacy. I heard these people describing many kinds of intimacy—touch, laughter, play, shared secrets, looking long into another's eyes, caring for the sick, standing with another beside the dying. There is the intimacy we enjoy with a lover, a friend, a child, a pet, a spouse, and even the stranger in the next seat whom we will never see again, and so we sometimes tell them things we've never told our husband or our wife.

As we talked, I began to see that nothing kills intimacy faster than the attempt to be intimate. Intimacy happens when you're not looking at each other, when you're attending to something else, such as washing the dishes, doing a puzzle, weeding the garden, scraping paint. As you tune into another reality, you tune into each other as well, and you see from the sides of your eyes how the other responds to the same thing that you respond to.

Perhaps that explains why we feel so close to others who pray. We are opening ourselves to the same reality, and later, when we talk about our prayers, we find that we have felt the same chagrin, frustration, longing, curiosity, and sometimes peace.

When I began my ministry and called on parishioners in the hospital, sometimes before I left I'd ask them if they would like me to pray. I was astonished at how often, men or women, they would break into tears and almost always say yes.

Prayer may be the act of ultimate intimacy because we open ourselves to the one before whom no sham, no posing, no dissembling is possible. Whatever we hide from each other, we cannot hide from God. That knowledge is no occasion for shame or fear. We trust that the one who has searched and known us knows and loves us better than we can know and love ourselves.

And when we feel that deep accepting love, which also judges us for every sin we have committed, we can reflect that love in our own lives, love ourselves better and others more wisely.

LOOK AND DO NOTHING

ON A RETREAT in 1992 I read an account by Father Pedro Arrupe, former head of the Jesuits, of his career as a priest. One story in particular jumped off the page at me.

Arrupe writes,

> I was once in Yamaguchi in charge of a group of boys and girls. Among these there was a girl of about twenty who without any pretense went regularly to the chapel and remained on her knees before the tabernacle—at times for hours on end.

> She seemed absorbed, as she remained there motionless. She was a charming and cheerful young woman and held in high esteem by her friends. I was struck with her persistent attendance at the chapel, and one day I made it a point to meet her as she was leaving.

> We began to speak as usual, and our conversation fell upon her constant and long visits to the Blessed Sacrament. I asked her, "And what do you

do in spending so much time before the tabernacle?" Without hesitation as if she were already prepared for my question, she gave me the unlikely answer, "Nothing." "What, nothing?" I asked "How is it possible for you to spend so much time there doing nothing?"

She seemed upset by my persistent questioning and she answered after a pause, "What do I do before the tabernacle? Well, I am there." And she was silent again, and we resumed our ordinary conversation.

Arrupe then points out to the reader that this young woman had stated the whole purpose of prayer in just a few words: "To be present before God." That is the essence of prayer beyond all words and actions, beyond all forms and customs. All these of course are the outward body of prayer, but the soul of prayer is presence before God.

The first act of prayer then is always invisible and inward attention to God. Because we are born with bodies, because our souls are housed in bodies, the inward action must always find an outward expression. We kneel or speak or sing or bow or finger beads, murmur a mantra, gaze at an icon or a flickering candle. But the essential act is attending to God.

That was the gift that Mary gave to Jesus—her attentiveness to God. That was the gift that the women gave to Jesus at the cross. That is the gift any and every worshipper can give to another, simply by attending and saying nothing.

Father John Vianney used to see an old man sitting in his parish church, sitting for hours in the late afternoon. Finally Vianney asked the old man what he was doing there. "I'm praying," said the old man. "And what do you say to God?" asked Vianney. "Oh, nothing," said the man, "I just look at him and he looks at me."

When we find it hard to pray, hard to continue, or hard even to begin, we can remember the model of the Japanese girl and the old French man. We can simply look and do nothing.

GOD IN THE DARKNESS

It happens to me usually when I have a bad cold. I'll wake up in the middle of the night with a stuffed head and a sore throat and, to quote the Lord Chancellor, a general sense that I haven't been sleeping in clover. And I realize that I won't be going to sleep again soon.

So I get up, put on my heavy bathrobe and slippers, and go downstairs, boil up the tea kettle, breathe steam for a while, put some Vicks on my throat, wrap it up in an old towel, take one decongestant pill, and then make myself a cup of strong tea laced with a bit of honey. I sit at the kitchen table and relax.

It's so pleasant, so cozy, to sit alone in the night, sometimes in darkness, and sip tea, and simply be. I often think of others who are up at that hour—nurses, watchmen, police, telephone operators, insomniacs, families by sickbeds, and taxi drivers. I feel close to these people. Sometimes I pray; sometimes I read a psalm; sometimes I just sit. But I always feel close to God.

I remembered this in church last Sunday morning when we came to that line in the psalm "I remember thy name in

the night, O Lord." (119:55) And then I remembered that other psalms speak of praying in the night. When I got home, I took down my concordance and wrote down all the night-praying lines I could find, such as:

"At midnight I will rise to give thee thanks." (119:62)

"Thou hast visited us in the night." (17:3)

"I call to remembrance my song in the night." (77:6)

"Commune with your own heart upon your bed." (149:5)

"I have cried before thee day and night." (88:1)

I found seventeen verses in all, and then in that very day's mail came this quotation from the newsletter of a Unitarian Universalist church in Worcester:

God is intimately tied to the night . . . [because] darkness reduces all things to their essence. Freed of vision, we see within. Primary concerns emerge. Much that seemed demanding and important is now a trick played by the light. . . . The depths night touches and the conflicts which it evokes in us produce the curious combination of fear, passion, intimacy, and mystery. God moves between the poles of . . . danger and promise. It is when the spirit is unable to forget itself by being lost in the day or distracted, that it must seep or seek. It is time to look for the God who walks within.

If you are blessed with the gift of going to bed early and rising early, you can get the same experience by rising in the dark, but that's a gift and not all of us have it.

God in the darkness. God in the night.

As the psalmist said elsewhere: "If I say surely the darkness shall cover, even the night shall be light about me. Yea, the darkness hideth not from thee, but the darkness and the light are both alike to thee." (139:11–12)

Amen to that.

THEY SHARED THEIR FAITH

I CAN'T REMEMBER where I saw it, but the poster was a beauty. At the top right, small white letters against a dark-blue background spelled the theme: "Religion in America 2000." From the top left side of the picture, a slender beam of white light cut downward across the dark-blue background, widening as it descended, and then halfway down the beam caught a white bird, flying across the great unknown. And that, said the poster, is what Religion in America 2000 will be about.

How curious, I thought. There goes Jonathan Livingston Seagull, the apotheosis of the journey into solitude—and the essence of American spirituality as we begin a new millennium. There's the gospel of Ralph Waldo Emerson, William James, Alfred North Whitehead, and the New Age gurus. Religion means: The alone flying into the alone. Questions occur to me when I see or hear that message. What about churches, synagogues, mosques, temples, meetinghouses? What about seminaries, conference centers, retreat houses, workshops, and university departments of religion?

What about abbeys and monasteries? What about choirs and prayer meetings? What about church suppers? What about soup kitchens? What about teachers, counselors, and spiritual directors?

What about the great traditions of religious thought? What about the history of our faith? What about Augustine, Aquinas, Maimonides, Rumi, Tagore, Thomas Merton, and Dorothy Day?

What about the countless ways in which we learn and share our faith with other human beings? What about the whole social fabric into which the threads of faith are woven? What about the Christ who came to people almost always in the presence of others and, with only two exceptions, never in their solitude?

So tell me, where does this one white bird of individualism come from? It comes from the American philosophers of individualism—in particular Emerson, who denied not only all intermediaries but the necessity of a faith community at all. It comes from Whitehead, who said that religion is what we do with our aloneness. It comes from James, who dismissed any consideration of communal religious experience in his classic *The Varieties of Religious Experience*.

Now, I prize solitude, and I know its value in the quest for God. I have been on a thirty-day silent retreat and spent most of each day alone. My daily prayers and my walks in nature take place in solitude. I read alone and I know it's essential for each pilgrim to face God by him or herself.

But solitude is less than half the story. We didn't learn our prayers, hymns, great texts and thoughts from our own selves. We learned them from teachers, preachers, mystics, prophets, philosophers, scholars, choir masters, spiritual directors, reformers, and writers, and countless men and women, most of whom were part of one religious community or another.

They shared their faith with us, blew on the spark within our soul, and fanned it into flames. When we fly alone, we do so only because of those who taught us.

I didn't learn Christ from myself. I learned Christ from community. Those who want to deepen their spiritual lives must sooner or later become part of a community.

SLEEP IN CHURCH

THERE'S A STORY in the Book of Acts about a young man named Eutychus, a resident of Troas. Eutychus went to hear a traveling preacher named Paul. The meeting was held in a rented room on the third floor of a building, and Eutychus must have arrived late because he had to take a seat at an open window.

The room was full, the hour late, and the service long. Paul was probably trying to describe everything that happened between creation and the last judgment. The flickering lamps by the speaker may have been hypnotic.

Eutychus fell first asleep and then out of the window. He must have hit the ground like a sack of cement because when the people rushed downstairs, they found him still as a stone, dead by all appearances.

Paul bent over him and said, "No, he's alive. He'll be fine."

Then everyone went back upstairs and had supper and talked until daybreak. And Eutychus eventually woke up and was fine. He went on to live an exemplary life. In fact, he became a saint and his feast day is August 24.

Now I like to think of Eutychus as the patron saint of those who fall asleep in church. I have a special fondness for these people because my first memories of church are memories of boredom and fatigue. When I became a minister of The First Parish of Sudbury, I looked with sympathy (maybe even envy) at my parishioner Al Haynes. "Hollywood Haynes," as we called him, fell asleep with almost mathematical precision three minutes into my sermons. I was glad that I could help him with a badly needed nap.

After all, we may learn more in sleep than waking. Think of the power of dreams. Think of the possibility of soft-spoken messages winging their way into our unconscious while we doze. Or think of the simple fact that someone sleeping is being quietly empowered to continue a day's work.

Why should everyone in church be awake? What a bore! Through how many sermons have I fought to stay conscious when the sensible thing would have been to surrender to the sea of forgetfulness rising within me, lay my head back into its warm, sustaining waters, and float on its gentle tides until the organ summoned me and countless others to wakefulness and the last hymn.

You may remember that Saint Theresa of Avila asked a group of novices what they should do if they were praying and found they had fallen asleep. The young women were embarrassed and no one answered. Theresa looked around at the silent class and said, "Would no one thank God?" Now that's the spirit of Christian gratitude.

I encourage you to sleep in church. A holy place is a good place to visit your unconscious. And if perchance to dream in a pew, might not that be, to paraphrase Freud, the royal road to the soul? Remember a good sermon is one from which you either arise inspired or awake refreshed.

Explain to your local priests or preachers that they shouldn't feel hurt or angry when they see your eyes slip shut and a beatific smile form on your lips. They should take it as a credit to the power of their eloquence that they have brought you into that sense of being held up by the everlasting arms, and that you are resting in that very place they are describing in their sermon.

For, as the psalmist says, "He giveth his beloved sleep." I'll close with a poem about sleep that my mother wrote:

Strong sleep that cuts an end to day,
that thrusts into oblivion
the disarray
of mask, trap, clutter;
that snaps in two the will to do,
twists the steel of scheme,
slams shut the door
to project, plan and plot.
Strange, then at dawn
a smile remains,
our love untouched.

PRAISE IN THIRTEEN STANZAS

I'VE READ many books by survivors of prison and death camps: *Night* by Elie Wiesel, *Man's Search for Meaning* by Victor Frankl, and *Survival in Auschwitz* by Primo Levi. I've read books on the history and evolution of these camps, on the psychology of the prisoners and the jailers, on the philosophical and theological issues of the holocaust. I have heard the voices of grief, rage, despair, courage, compassion, and even denial, but never until last fall had I heard a single voice of praise coming out of these camps.

My friend and colleague Terry Burke gave me a few photocopied sheets of paper entitled "Akathist: Glory to God for All Things." It was a poem of praise to God divided into thirteen stanzas. It was strong and charming.

O God, how lovely to be your guest, breezes full of scents, mountains reaching to the skies, waters like a boundless mirror. . . . All nature murmurs mysteriously, breathing depths of tenderness, birds and beasts of the forest bear the imprint of your love. . . . In the land where beauty does not grow old rings out the cry 'Alleluia.'

I read on:

The dark storm clouds of life bring no terror to those in whose hearts your fire burns brightly. Outside is the darkness of the whirlwind, the terror and howling of the storm, but in the heart, in the presence of Christ, there is light and peace, silence. The heart sings: 'Alleluia.'

I read all thirteen stanzas, knowing nothing of who wrote it or where it was written until I came to the end and found the following words: "This akathist was composed by protopresbyter Gregory Petrov in prison camp shortly before his death."

Petrov had taken the title from a poem written by Saint John Chrysostom during his exile and just before his death in 407. Later I learned that Gregory Petrov was a priest in the Russian Orthodox Church and possibly a science teacher as well, who died in a Soviet labor camp in 1940. He must have written this psalm of praise on scraps of paper and given them to a fellow Christian, who may have passed it on to others, until eventually his poem left the prison and found its way into the hands of the Orthodox faithful. Eventually it came to America in an English translation.

"If I descend into hell, behold thou art there," said the psalmist. Gregory Petrov knew this and told us what that meant in the year of our Lord 1940. Only once in this poem does he mention his imprisonment. In the third stanza he wrote, "When the lightning flash has lit up the camp dining-hall, how feeble seems the light from the lamp." Other than that he never suggests the suffering and evil from which he writes, so filled with praise was he.

Gregory Petrov is one more Christian witness among thousands who give us courage and renew our faith. His poem joins us, the fainthearted, to the choir of angels and the communion of saints who praise God in heaven, on earth, and even in hell.

GOD'S SECOND JOKE

SOME YEARS AGO I heard Robert Frost read his poetry at the Lincoln Town Hall. One short poem went like this:

> Lord, if you'll forgive all the little jokes I've
> played on thee,
> I'll forgive the great big one you played on me.

Everyone laughed, and Robert Frost said, "People always laugh when I read that poem, and I wonder what they think was the great big joke God played on them."

Sometimes we feel that God, or life, or Fate has played a joke on us—a bad joke, such as the time we trusted a partner and he or she let us down, or when we worked hard on a new business and it failed, or when we hoped and prayed for a good cause, and a new president sent it down the tubes. Through most of our life we've made up our own list of God's Bad Jokes. In the Bible God often jokes by letting someone build up his estate, business, or sense of self-importance, and then, *boom!* It collapses, explodes, or implodes. Jesus once described the divine turnaround with these words: "Those who are first will be last, and those who are last will be first."

We sing of that theme in a chant called the *Magnificat* on Sunday mornings, a song that Mary sings when she's heard news of her pregnancy. She sings, "He has brought down the mighty from their thrones and has lifted up the lowly. He has filled the hungry with good things and he has sent the rich away empty."

Psalm 2 describes God watching and laughing at kings who set themselves against the righteous. The psalm says "He holds them in derision" before he unleashes his wrath.

The Bible tells us of another kind of joke God plays on us—a joke, he plays when we are down and out, dejected, lost, without hope or vision. At such times, we don't know where we're going or how we'll get there. At such times, scripture tells us, God surprises us and shows us a way, gives us courage, lifts our hearts, and helps us take the next few steps.

As the *Magnificat* says, "He has helped his servant," or as the psalmist says, "I believe that I shall see the goodness of the Lord in the land of the living."

God's second joke is the raising of our sight, the raising of our spirits, the raising of our sense of his love for us. That is a joke that heals, that helps, that takes us through the next hour, day, week, year, and who knows, perhaps the next life as well.

That's the divine comedy Dante wrote of. That is the laughter of the angels. That is joy, which is the best joke of all.

WORDS THAT ARE YOURS

WE DID SOMETHING very old-fashioned with the children in our church one year. We made them memorize the 121st psalm—you know, the one that begins "I will lift up mine eyes unto the hills. From whence cometh my help? My help cometh from the Lord who made heaven and earth."

They all memorized it, their parents too, and we said the psalm together when we worshipped on Sunday mornings. Everyone chimed in. It was a great sound. I think the children were proud of themselves. I should add, they also learned the Lord's Prayer and the Collect for Grace and the Versicles and the Alleluia. They did pretty well, even if we were a bit old-fashioned.

We were deliberate about this, of course. We believed that if you have memorized something and have a feeling for it, it belongs to you. You don't need a book or a computer screen in order to say it. It's yours at any time of day or night.

An actor or actress may read their lines from a script at the first rehearsal, but only after they know the lines can they create the character they portray. Only then can they make the part their own.

And so it is with the congregation. Although almost everyone holds the prayer book open during the service, most of the people who have worshipped at King's Chapel for more than a year or two know the service by heart. It's their service. That's why we call our prayer book *The Book of Common Prayer*.

And when we're off on a trip or alone in our room or walking the street, we can say the Collect for Grace or Peace, we can sing the *Te Deum*, we can murmur the prayer of confession, and a piece of us has gone to church wherever we are. That's not bad, you know.

A Unitarian colleague of mine, a minister from Canada, wrote me of visiting a patient in the hospital, a woman who could say only a very few words, one of which was *sin*, for this woman was overwhelmed by guilt. She said the word *sin* over and over again. One day she said to my friend, "Pray for me." My friend, whose parishioners usually do not ask or want him to pray with them or for them or near them, stumbled through an extemporaneous prayer.

When he finished, he paused and during that pause this woman who could utter only a few words, began to say the Lord's Prayer. My friend joined her in that prayer and they said it together very slowly.

He wrote to me,

It was amazing that she could say the prayer given that she had such difficulty with single words. We said it over and over again for much of the afternoon. Despite her difficulties, she was able to reach deep down inside herself and bring forth those familiar and beloved words. It was a holy moment.

That prayer belonged to the woman. At some point in her life she had memorized it. It is old-fashioned, but it still works and you don't have to be in a nursing home or a hospital to know the blessings of owning a prayer or a psalm or a poem or anything that's meaningful to you. It's yours for the memorizing.

OUR DESIRE FOR GOD

OUR DESIRE FOR GOD

"SELF-KNOWLEDGE," said novelist John Barth, "is always bad news." Freud never put it so bluntly, but his exploration of the mind uncovered far more prisons, torture chambers, freaks, and monsters, than it did green pastures and innocents. Freud and John Barth suggest that the depths of the soul are dark and devious, that the human heart is greedy, that we are good through force and fear.

I was therefore struck by Saint Paul writing to the Christians in Romans (chapter 7), "I do not do what I want but I do the very thing I hate. I want to do good but in practice I do evil." Paul, supposedly the dour disciple, is saying that he, and therefore you and I, really want good. He says that by our nature we desire good.

Paul thinks better of you and me than do the novelists, psychologists, and economists of our times. And so does Saint Ignatius Loyola. When he taught his earliest disciples, he continually asked them, "What do you desire?" And he pressed that question because he believed that beneath their more immediate desires for food, clothing, shelter, love, and power lay their deepest desire for God.

He believed that they desired God because they knew instinctively that God was the center of their life. Because this desire for God was our deepest desire, Loyola thought that either the satisfaction or frustration of our more immediate desires could lead us to God.

This is a far cry from the religious suspicion in which I was raised, a world that assumed that what you wanted was probably wrong simply because you wanted it.

If we are images of God, then we carry within us the desire to know God, and this desire reflects God's glory to this world. During our service each Sunday I read the following prayer:

> Almighty God who hast given us grace at this time with one accord to make our common supplications unto thee, and hast promised by thy beloved Son that where two or three are gathered together in his name thou wilt grant their requests, fulfill now, O Lord, the desires and petitions of thy servants as may be most expedient for them.

We pray to a God who trusts our deepest desire because God knows that this desire will lead us to his truth, his peace, his justice. It's curious that in a world that has urged us to free ourselves from the church, the synagogue, the meetinghouse, the mosque, and religion itself, in a world that enslaves us in its deterministic, dark philosophies, it is the communities of faith that remind us that we are free souls in a fallen world and chosen, if we choose, to dance in praise of that One whom we desire above all else.

BACH'S OWN FAITH

WE WHO LOVE the work of Bach forget sometimes how hard a life he had. He worked with difficult patrons, stingy rectors, inept soloists, and rebellious instrumentalists.

He struggled to support his wife and eleven children (they lost another ten at birth.) To make ends meet, he ran a choir school for sixty unruly boys. He might have starved, he said, were it not for the funeral and wedding fees. He failed to land the big job at the Jacobskirche in Hamburg and was third choice for the Thomaskirche in Leipzig. During his lifetime he was considered by other musicians as a throwback to old musical styles.

Bach said almost nothing in his letters or diary about his own faith, and we knew little of it until 1933. In that year a Lutheran pastor from Detroit spent a night at the home of a local farmer, who showed his pastor an old German Bible his father had bought in Philadelphia in 1847. The pastor saw Bach's signature on the front page of this Bible and knew he had a treasure. He took the Bible home to study and in the Bible's margins found Bach's commentary on scripture.

Beside First Chronicles chapter 25, where King David assigns the singers and players their parts in the temple worship, Bach wrote, "This chapter is the true foundation of all church music pleasing to God."

Beside First Chronicles 28, verse 21, Bach wrote, "A magnificent proof that . . . music has been ordained by David through the spirit of God."

Second Chronicles 5, verse 13 reads, "And it came to pass as the trumpeters and singers were as one to make one sound to be heard praising and thanking the Lord, and when they lifted up their voices with the trumpets and cymbals and instruments, and praised the Lord, saying, 'For his mercy endureth for ever', then the house was filled with a cloud . . . for the glory of the Lord had filled the house of God." Beside this Bach wrote, "At a reverent performance of music, God is ever present in his mercy."

Bach did not need words to explain his faith. He had said it all in his music. If you have heard the Credo from the *B Minor Mass*, or the "Come ye daughters" from the *St. Matthew Passion*, or "Christians, be joyful" from the *Christmas Oratorio*, you will know that for Bach, God was ever present in the faithful performance of his work.

He fought parsons, patrons, and bad musicians. He wrote and rehearsed endlessly. He worked himself blind, and he did this not just to support himself and family and not to achieve a fame that he never expected. He wrote, rehearsed, and conducted for the God who was his ultimate audience. Because of Bach's faith, we are his debtors and his grateful listeners.

BOTH MAN AND GOD

SOME MONTHS AGO I watched a video of a BBC program about a biblical scholar who had studied the Dead Sea Scrolls for some years and decided that the scrolls destroyed the authority for Christianity. He thought they proved that Christianity was a secret Jewish cult and not a new religion.

The BBC program was facile, simplistic, entertaining, and memorable. That should not surprise us. Television does not deal well with complexity, and most viewers want an easy summary of an issue.

As I watched this program and saw gross misstatements of fact and radical oversimplifications, I grew angry. By the end I could scarcely conceal my irritation from those with whom I watched it. But I was angry about more than met the eye. I had to see the book on which this program was based. So I took it out and read the introduction.

In the last sentence I saw the assumption that disturbed me. The author said that if we want to make Jesus more "human and accessible," then we may have to sacrifice his divinity to his humanity. "No," I said to myself, "that you can't do. At least the church can't make that sacrifice."

Now you may wonder why I reacted so strongly. After all, you might be thinking, "Don't we want a more human Jesus? Don't we want a Jesus who shares our tears, our hunger, our anxiety, our sleeplessness, our backaches, and our yearning for something more? Don't we want a Christ who is one with us in our humanity? Because if he is not part of us, then he's just up there in heaven and who cares?"

And I say, right. Right as far as it goes, but it doesn't go far enough. Of course, we want a Jesus who was and is human. The author of the Letter to the Hebrews says, "We have not a high priest who is unable to sympathize with us in our weakness, but who was tempted in all ways as we are, save without sinning."

A human Jesus? Yes. But not *just* a human Jesus. If Jesus is *only* human, then he becomes only Marlon Brando in *On the Waterfront*, or the neurotic teenager of the Leonard Bernstein *Mass*, or the Pied Piper of *Jesus Christ Superstar*. If Jesus is only human, then he is one more hero in a long line of heroes. He has no power to transform, enlighten, save us. He's one more fallible ideal.

Only fifteen years after the crucifixion, St. Paul wrote, "From now on we see Jesus no more simply as a human; but from now on if any one is in Jesus, he is in a new creation." To be the bridge between heaven and earth, Jesus

228

must be both human and divine. The Council of Chalcedon was very clear on that in 451 A.D., and it's still true today. Jesus is both man and mystery, both of us and above us, both divine and daily in his doings.

Both natures must be present if Christ is to have power and presence in our lives. Jesus danced the delicate dance between heaven and earth—a man of sweat and tears and blood and sorrows and laughter, but also a man of judgment, mercy, mystery, and absolute obedience to a law and a voice and a word above all laws, voices, and words.

Only if Jesus is of both worlds can he be significant.

ERIC LIDDELL'S FINEST HOUR

A GOOD MANY of you have probably seen the award-winning film *Chariots of Fire*. It is the story of two British runners who won gold medals in the 1924 Olympics. The one who interested me was the devout young Scot, who refused to run his regular event, the 100-meter dash, because the trials were to be held on Sunday, and he would take part in no athletic events on the Lord's Day.

So he trained for and ran the four hundred–meter event and, as I said, won the gold medal at the Paris Olympics. The movie ends there. As the screen goes dark, white words appear on it telling us "Eric Liddell died in China on February 21, 1944."

"Died in China in 1944?" I thought. "He might have died in a Japanese internment camp." I called my brother: "Was there a guy named Liddell in our camp?"

"Yeah," he said, "a runner."

The Olympic victory was only the beginning of Liddell's career. In the next year, 1925, he went to China and taught chemistry and math in a missionary high school in Tianjin. After six years, he went back to

Scotland and was ordained as a minister, returned to China, became engaged, and waited three years for his fiancé to finish her nurse's training in Toronto. After three years of happy married life, Liddell was asked by the mission board to go into the countryside west of Tianjin to preach, baptize, marry, organize schools and churches, and visit and encourage the scattered Christians there. This countryside was a dangerous place to go in 1938. Chinese and Japanese troops were fighting for the same space. There was shelling, rape, executions, poverty. It was no place for a foreign family, so Liddell's wife and children stayed in Tianjin.

Liddell spent three hard years in that territory until 1941, when war broke out with the Allied powers. Liddell, a Scot in Japanese-occupied China, was sent to a civilian concentration camp in northern China. (His family had previously returned to Canada.) He became an important person in that camp, but in his own quiet way.

He lived in a men's dormitory and was in charge of Blocks 23 and 24, with over 230 single men and women. He taught a Bible class. He performed uncounted acts of kindness for old or sick folk in the camp, fetching their water, food, and coal. A Russian prostitute said he was the only one in camp who did her a favor without receiving payment in kind. Above all, he devoted himself to the young people of the camp—coaching and refereeing their hockey and soccer games, mending their broken hockey sticks, spending evenings with them in the game room, playing chess, or directing a square dance.

He still refused to take part in Sunday sports. One day some teenagers in his charge rebelled and organized their own game on a Sunday afternoon. It ended in a fight. They decided to meet again on the next Sunday afternoon, either to play or to fight. Eric Liddell heard about it. When the two teams met the next Sunday, Eric Liddell walked onto the field. The man who refused to run on Sunday in order to win a gold medal was willing to referee on Sunday in order to keep peace among a group of frustrated teenagers.

In the fall of that year, 1944, Liddell began to slow down. He had headaches. He was tired. For the first time in his life he was depressed. On February 21, he was lying on his bed and wrote on a scrap of paper the first line of his favorite hymn, "Be still, my soul, the Lord is on thy side." He got up and went to the game room to visit the young people.

Suddenly he was seized with a spasm of coughing and choking. He was taken to the hospital and died shortly thereafter from a brain tumor. At the memorial service, they sang his favorite hymn, "Be still, my soul."

Eric Liddell's finest hour was, I think, not in Paris in 1924, but at Wehsien concentration camp on a Sunday afternoon in 1944. He was a true disciple.

NEVER FAR FROM HOME

GEOGRAPHY FIRST. Nineveh is five hundred miles east of Israel. Tarshish is due west by two thousand miles. God told Jonah to go to Nineveh. He booked passage on a ship for Tarshish.

We remember Jonah because we are Jonah. The word of the Lord comes to us saying, "Love your enemy," "Take up your bed and walk," "Leave home," "Go home," "Lose yourself," and we head in the opposite direction.

We may find ourselves saying, like Moses when God called him to lead his tribe, "Try my brother, Lord. He talks real good." Unlike the obedient Isaiah, we may say: "Here am I Lord, but send someone else. Send my brother, my partner, my colleague, send anyone but me. I'm not into self-sacrifice this year. I'm burned out. I need a vacation, not a vocation. I think I'll head for Tarshish." Tarshish is a tempting place. It's always two thousand miles from where we should be going.

Notice that after God ordered Jonah to Nineveh, Jonah didn't argue. He didn't refuse or get angry. He just sailed off in the opposite direction, a classic passive-aggressive. He avoided not just God's word, but God as well, and he left without a murmur.

God bless the atheists! At least they argue. At least they complain. At least they question. Like Job (and as God says at the end of that story) they are closer to God than those who offer cheap explanations for life's injustice.

It is the silent leave we take from God that hurts us most—the agnostic indifference, the passionless disinterest that cools the soul and quiets the mind with measurable benefits until suddenly we are plunged into the soul's dark night, when a good friend dies in a car crash, an infant is stillborn, our life savings vanish in one bad investment, the firm collapses, the doctor murmurs on seeing a gray spot on the X-ray.

Suddenly, angry and aware, we find ourselves once again in God's perplexing presence and far from the beaches and bistros of Tarshish.

I know from my own life that no one can forget God faster than a minister. Heavens, I say to myself, if I am talking God-talk, I must be God's servant. Well, no—no more, no less, than any other.

The word of the Lord came to Jonah, and he took a ship and headed for the sunset instead of the sunrise. The world is filled with emigrés like Jonah, sipping tequila at little tin tables on dusty streets, wiping glasses behind the bar, making bricks for Pharaoh, tending pigs in the local hog farm—men and women far from home but despite the distance never far from God; never far from God's call to come home and become themselves again, the men or women they were meant to be.

For here's the hell of that half-escape. It never works. We flee God's word, and we flee his mercy. We flee his command, and we flee his forgiveness. We flee his presence, and we flee his love.

That's easy to do when you're young and tough and have a world before you, a world to conquer and command. But the day comes when the heart's hunger wells so huge that we become one vast ache and then it's time to head for home, no longer a place now but a condition, something like peace. At sixty, I think I understand this.

The good news is: We cannot escape.

In our geography Tarshish may be two thousand miles west of Nineveh, but in God's geography they are next-door neighbors in the vast metropolis of his kingdom. The bar and the pigsty and the brickyard and the little tin table are not in hell but purgatory. They are stopping places on the way to heaven.

The ache in the heart and the hunger for home and the sour stink of the whale's belly are scenes from God's divine comedy in which we play our clumsy parts and through which we will at last come home. And the presence of the Lord that we tried to flee is everywhere, in the first act and the last. As the psalmist said, "Though I take the wings of the morning and dwell in the uttermost parts of the sea, even there shall thy hand lead me and thy right hand shall hold me."

GIVE ME JESUS

It was the same old tease and I fell for it, as I had fallen so many times before. This time it was a book written by a journalist about his walk along the pilgrim route from southern France to the church of Saint James in Santiago de Compostela. The book taught me something about the history of the road and too much about the writer and his companions..

When I'd finished the book, I realized that I was waiting to see if he had changed because of his journey, his conversations, his prayers and thoughts, the sights along the road, and his experience at the shrine itself. I wondered if he knew himself better because of his pilgrimage. I wasn't looking for a conversion or even a transformation. I just wondered if he felt close to those who had walked the road before him.

Well, he wasn't. By the end he was still the half-spiritual, half-cynical seeker, and the book was one more book about the quest that never goes anywhere, but on.

The bumper sticker says "The Journey Is the Answer." Yeah, right. I should have known better.

Like so many of my peers, bored with church, dull preaching, and platitudes, I've gone out looking for God in places and people who seemed more promising than the tried, the true, and the tired old ways.

I've gone to the prayer breakfast that was more breakfast than prayer and more talk than prayer or breakfast. I went to the Science and Religion conferences on Star Island where we mere mortals watched in awe while Harlow Shapley reviewed his doubts.

I went to something called "An Evening with God" with Harvey Cox and Joni Mitchell and a communion service that didn't quite come off, since there was too much bread and not enough wine. I've read far too many articles in *Time*, *Newsweek,* and *The Atlantic*, articles about prayer, miracles, Jesus, God, angels, all of which ended with a thundering "Maybe." Always the tease and nothing at the end—no clothes, no emperor, only the crowd waiting as usual for something to happen to somebody else.

Jesus saw the people leaving him for a more promising speaker, and he turned to the twelve and asked, "Will you too leave me?" And Peter answered: "Lord, to whom can we go? You have the words of eternal life."

Peter's words make sense only if you've tried a lot of other things and realized that they couldn't deliver. Only then do we look for one who not only speaks the truth but is the truth, one who is not just truth articulate but truth incarnate. That truth we find at the grave, the cross, the altar, the Bible, and where- and whenever God's people gather.

Two years ago in a West Indian chapel, I heard a song I won't forget.

In the morning when I rise
in the morning when I rise
in the morning when I rise,
give me Jesus.
Give me Jesus,
give me Jesus.
You can have all the world,
Give me Jesus.

That says it for me. Give me Jesus.

GRAFFITI

SOME THINGS make life interesting—like graffiti. By graffiti I mean any kind of unofficial public messages, whether on bumper stickers, posters, T-shirts, buttons, tattoos, the walls of abandoned buildings, or the sides of subway cars. Graffiti are a great means of public communication, because their only sponsor is a solitary soul.

Of course, we have the predictable inscriptions— "Ronnie Loves Rita" in bright-red paint sprayed on a highway overpass, "Let Go and Let God" on the church sign board, "Kiss Me, I'm Irish" on the Saint Patrick's Day T-shirts. But I'm amazed at the variety and significance of messages beyond these.

Drawn in pencil on the stone floor of a church courtyard in Santorini were the words of Alfred J. Prufrock, "I have measured out my life in coffee spoons." In the year that Che Guevara was killed, the words, "Che Lives," appeared on a rock in the college square of my alma mater. Neatly lettered on the granite entrance to the Park Street Station in downtown Boston were the words: "God is dead, Nietsche." Below it someone had written, "Nietsche is dead, God." On a yellow T-shirt worn by a young man walking into the Charles Street stop, I saw the sad words "Born to Lose." And on the walls of the catacombs of San Sebastian in Rome, I saw written in the common Greek of the first century these words: "Paul and Peter, Pray for Victor." Who was Victor? Whom was he fleeing when he came to the catacombs? And what happened to him?

Behind each inscription, declaration, and confession lies a human being who somehow sums up him- or herself for us. They touch us with their brief words.

The most terrible thing for anyone is not to be known. That's why we put bumper stickers on our car that identify us to other commuters who will never know our name or face or soul. We advertise that "We Brake for Whales," or that "My Son Made the Honor Roll at Tuckerman High." "One Day at a Time" we caution other drivers, or "Honk if You Love Jesus."

We wear T-shirts that tell others "I'd Rather Be Dancing," "Arms Are for Hugging," "Rock Is Real," "Glad to Be Gay," "Greek and Proud of It."

None of us can survive in an impersonal world. Each of us needs to be known, to know others. And that I suppose—from our human perspective—is why we assume that God also needs to be known and needs to know us.

Of course, our need does not create a truth. Everyone at some point or other must make an assumption about the nature of this universe. With Jews and Christians and others, I assume that God has left His signature in this world so that we can know something about Him. We read that signature at the ocean's edge, at the mountain-top, at the break of day, and on the pages of holy scripture. We read it in our heart's longing and the promises of our traditions.

We Christians read it in the life and death and rebirth of a wandering rabbi and in the family that bears his name. We read this signature because we can bear any loneliness except the loneliness of being ultimately alone. We must have a companion in this cosmos. We must have a friend during our brief visit in time who answers to our call. We need to know the one who called us into being.

And that is why we read God's graffiti on rocks and T-shirts, on sacred writ, in bread and wine, and in our inmost hearts. We can see these because we ourselves are God's signature in this world.

ALLEE ALLEE HOME FREE!

IT WAS A summer evening, and my wife and I were sitting on a park bench with maybe a hundred others—young, old, black, white, Chinese, Hispanic, upper-crust, down and out; all of us listening to a five-piece band—drum, sax, trumpet, clarinet, and trombone. They were playing the Golden Oldies from the 1940s: "Muskrat Ramble," "Tuxedo Junction," "String of Pearls," "In the Mood."

It was a great hour, and for the last number they cut loose on "When the Saints Come Marching In." They weren't halfway through, and the trumpet was just beginning to take off in what they'd call "a cadenza" in Symphony Hall, when the manager came to the microphone—a gray-haired fellow with his shirt hanging out in back.

The band stopped playing and the manager said, "Seems like a lady here has lost a couple of children and she'd like your help. Their names are. . . " He paused and turned to the mother behind him. "Sophie. Sophie and Lily. So if any of you see them . . ."

The mother came up to mike and began to speak. "They're three and five. Sophie has a brown dress, and

Lily has white shorts and a dark-blue jumper. Please look around you."

Suddenly the crowd was serious. The players looked worried, the manager scowled, and the mother was in tears. After all, this was a city park, and it was past ten o'clock. Strange people roamed these parks at night, and two lost girls might not be safe.

People began to call their names, "Sophie," "Lily." Some left the crowd to poke about the trees and bushes. There were murmurs and anxious looks. Suddenly two little girls came running to their mother by the microphone, the manager signaled to the band. The drummer picked up the beat, the trumpet picked up the cadenza, and the crowd clapped and cheered while the mother tried to hug two small girls at the same time.

This happened in New York City last summer, but it's the oldest story in the world: the story of lost and found. It's the story of the Prodigal Son and Peek-a-Boo and the Blue Bird and Persephone. It's our story too because we all want to be found.

First we hide. Everyone does, I don't know why. Perhaps it's part of growing up. We have to hide to find out who we are. We hid from our parents when we were teenagers.

"How was school today?"

"Fine."

Fine. It could have been marvelous, it could have been terrible, but we all said, "Fine." We hid from our teachers, our priests and pastors, bosses, colleagues, even our friends. We hid from God by living as if we existed in isolation.

In hiding we began to find out who we were. We had to do that. Everyone does. But then there came a point when we wanted to be found, but all we knew was how to hide. And so we had to come out of our hiding places.

Robert Frost wrote about that:

> But so with all that play at hide-and-seek to God
>   afar,
> So all who hide too well away must speak and
>   tell us where they are.

Allee, allee, home free! Now that's good news.

GOD'S PRESENCE

SPEAKING OF SPIRITUALITY, maybe Christians should stop speaking of spirituality. Prayer, yes; contemplation, yes; conversion, yes; transformation, yes. But spirituality? I think not. Why? Because by now spirituality means almost anything, and therefore it means nothing.

For example, I heard a story about Elvis Presley's one big spiritual experience that appears in David Guralnik's biography of him. It seems that Elvis and his sidekick Larry Geller were driving across the Nevada desert when Elvis looked up and saw a cloud that looked to him like the head of Joseph Stalin. This was in the 1950s when Stalin was Satan.

Presley was troubled by the sight of Joseph Stalin in the clouds, but as he drove on and watched the cloud, it changed under the changing wind (or was it the Holy Spirit?) into a likeness of Jesus. Or so Elvis Presley thought. At this point Presley told Geller that he was going to become a monk. His resolution cooled as they got closer to Las Vegas, and after the two arrived, they went on about their business and made a less-than-glorious movie called *Harem Scarem*. So much for life transforming experiences.

Admittedly, I've put my point in the extreme. But my question is this: If the word *spirituality* can describe this kind of experience and almost any kind of experience that is relaxing, pleasant, centering, or upbeat, experiences such as walking your dog, strolling on the beach, or listening to Brahms, if all these things and many more mean spiritual, I think I have a right to ask if we should use that word to describe our relationship to God, our dependence on God and the claims God puts on our lives.

I don't for a moment doubt that God can speak to us while we are exercising our dog, walking the beach, or hearing Brahms. God may speak to us through pleasant experiences. We don't have to live on carrot sticks and wear a hair shirt to know the Lord. But on the other hand we'd be ridiculous to assume that any striking, dramatic, or pleasant experience is a sign of God's presence.

Spiritual is a popular word because it describes an experience that comes to us as individuals. In the spirit of good old American Ralph Waldo Emerson, it implies that you don't need a community, a church, a mosque, a sangha, or the synagogue to grow in the knowledge of God. And that's the kind of religious individualism I question.

Of course God speaks to us personally. Of course God comes to us in solitude. Alfred North Whitehead was partly right when he said, "Religion is what we do with our solitude." But we would never have these individual experiences of God if we had not been taught and encouraged and led and directed by others. Without communities of faith, religion would be a perennial mist—without force and, I suspect, without a future.

We have faith because there are communities of faith. Within these communities we find teachers, mentors, congregations, and companions on the path to God. Without these we never grow.

You can play the piano without a teacher and without music and without ever hearing the work of others, but I'm not sure anyone else would want to hear what you were playing, and I wonder if you'd even stay interested yourself.

And that is why you drive to church to play the organ, rehearse the choir, sing, usher, prepare to preach or celebrate the Eucharist. Your community is the occasion for God's presence.

Maybe Elvis should have joined that monastery. Strange as it may sound, he might have found a deeper joy than he ever found in drugs or drink or maybe even rock and roll.

THE LIGHT OF THE WORLD

WE WERE TALKING one night at supper when I learned that one of our party grew up in Alaska, in Anchorage.

"What is it like there?" I asked.

"Dark," she said. "In the winter, the sun comes up at ten-thirty and it's down by two in the afternoon. You get up in the dark and go to bed in the dark. You go to school in the dark and come home in the dark.

"And how does that affect people?" I asked.

"It makes them strange," she said. "Really strange. There's a lot of drinking, a lot of crime. And at any given time, almost one percent of the population of Alaska will be in the state mental hospitals. You really ought to come out and visit," she added. "In the summer."

I declined. But what she said reminded me of something I saw on television about people who become very depressed unless they have sunlight. They suffer terrible depression in the winter unless they can be exposed to intense artificial light that seems to affect them as sunlight does and produces some kind of chemical change within their bodies. The light cheers them up.

That may be true of all of us. We need light, not for illumination or photosynthesis, but more simply, we need light. And that may explain our uneasiness as autumn ends and the first snow falls in early November, when our fall chores are not quite finished. We have yet to gather wood, pull down the storm windows, and take out the winter coats. We follow the autumn rituals with a certain apprehension. It is not only cold we fear. We don't like darkness either.

That is why we keep our ritual lights—lamps, candles, what have you—and set them flickering, warm and fascinating, in the center of the dining table, on the mantelpiece, in the window, on our desks, wherever we need reminders that light will return. That is why we have logs in the fireplace and burn them as an emblem of the season that, even now, we look forward to, when the great sun will bathe our towns, our fields, and our bodies in the natural sacrament of healing.

Jesus called himself the light of the world. He knew, of course, what darkness was, the darkness of history and the darkness of the human heart. He knew that Roman cruelty, human greed, natural poverty, and the long, long wait for the Messiah's coming had bred in his people an anger, a despair, a hopelessness, in some, a madness, as terrible as any winter of twenty-hour nights and four-hour days.

He knew that darkness drove some to violence and others to impotence. He knew that many could not believe that day would ever come. And when he called himself the light, he knew his people's frustration and anger would leap out like lightning against him. For his presumption, for his hope, for his promise that, in fact, the day was breaking even then and that he was like the morning star that heralded its advent. He knew that many could believe no more; history had been so cruel for so long. But he knew that, perhaps, a few would believe and that those who trusted the return of light would be the one's to confirm the kingdom's coming.

He calls himself the light, his life the light, his death the light, his resurrection light, clear and pale, like the fine illumination in a Wyeth winter painting. He promises us still that the day will return and that those who trust the light will, in the long run, be the happiest of all.

JESUS NOW AND THEN

SOME YEARS AGO, a Quaker named Henry Cadbury taught New Testament at Harvard Divinity School. He had written a number of books and was known throughout the country for his scholarship. A friend of mine tells me that one day he came home after completing the manuscript for a new book and said to his wife, "I've thought of the title. I'm going to call it 'Jesus, Then and Now.' "

Cadbury's wife replied, "You'd better be careful, Henry. Jesus then and now is likely to become Jesus now and then."

When I first heard that story I thought, "Clever!" But then I began to think, "That's more than clever. It's true. That is what happens to Jesus among liberal Protestants."

You may not realize it but in the 1800s, biblical scholars had high hopes of discovering who the *real* Jesus was and what could be known of him with historical accuracy. These scholars spoke with scorn of the Jesus of faith and contrasted that figure with their supposedly more rational Jesus of history.

At this point, Albert Schweitzer was still studying for

his doctorate in theology and read these "historical" accounts of Jesus. He came to the conclusion that it was impossible to write a historical account of Christ. Here's how he put it:

> The study of the life of Jesus has had a curious history. It set out believing that it could bring Him straight into our times as teacher and savior. It rejoiced to see life and movement coming into the figure once more and this historical Jesus advancing, as it seemed, to meet us. But He does not stay; He passes by our time and returns to His own. What surprised and dismayed the theologians was that they could not keep Him in our time and had to let Him go into His own.

Those who pin their faith on the historical Jesus of the last century will find themselves without a Jesus in this one. In the long run it is not the historical figure who is important. What is important is the vision, power, and faith that came through this man to his followers. What is ultimately important is not his person but his presence. To his disciples and to their converts, his presence was the presence of God. This presence did not die with him but created the Christian church and enabled it to survive disappointment, confusion, corruption, and compromise.

Despite its betrayals of the gospel, despite its fear and compromise, despite its greed and cruelty, the church is still the bearer of this presence and this promise to this world, not the man called Jesus but the presence called

Christ. That is why the church is called not the Jesus church but the Christian church.

What the church claims (and I must admit that it's a huge claim) is that the power and faith and vision that lived in this Jew from Nazareth are available to us through the scripture, sacraments, and fellowship in the Christian church today.

Through these realities I have been sustained and encouraged and challenged by a power that comes not from God directly to me as an isolated individual, but from God through His community to me.

This community has taught me how to sing, how to pray, how to read scripture, how to worship, how to work with groups of people, and how to be alone with God. It is the community that bears this presence, and I know God's presence only through these people.

It is not a case of Jesus now and then. Rather, it is a case of Christ now as then, or as the writer of Hebrews put it, "Jesus Christ the same yesterday and today and forever." Such, if I understand it correctly, is the faith of the church.

A SIMPLER LIFE

I WAS BROWSING through the library of a retreat center in Florida when I came across a book of excerpts from the writings of George MacDonald, a Scottish pastor who was kicked out of his first church and who then supported his wife and eleven children by writing children's stories.

One quote struck me with particular power. He said, "It may be infinitely less evil to murder a man than to refuse to forgive him. One assault kills the body. The other kills the soul." Jesus said, "Do not fear those who kill the body and not the soul."

Isn't that just what rape is? It assaults not just a precious body, the once-safe boundaries, of another person, but rape assaults the integrity, safety, and centeredness of the victim as well. The rapist invades interior as well as exterior space. He attacks and sometimes kills a soul. I have talked to women who remember being raped, and years later the act is still devastating, far beyond the violation of their body.

Rape is not the only act that kills the soul.

I think of the young men working in one particular hot-shot company where they are asked and taught to lie, not just to their customers, but to each other as well. They do this for the sake of annual salaries in six figures, and all the time (they'd laugh if they read this) they are losing their souls. They are destroying their own integrity and centeredness.

The horror of the death camps is not only in the millions starved, tortured, and killed, but the crushing of those souls who after a time dared not to even think of resistance and learned to fear death more than misery. It was the prisoners' fear of death that made them tractable, for once infected with this fear, they would do anything to postpone a trip to the gas chambers. The Nazis killed souls as well as bodies.

We live in a world that conspires to attack and destroy our souls, to convince us that we have no soul, to delude us into thinking that the evening news is reality and that salvation lies in the next holiday sale. When we count ourselves so cheap that we imagine a Caribbean vacation or a new doodad will bring us happiness, then we have lost our sense of soul. For all intents and purposes, it has died.

When I think of Henry Thoreau living his two years of simplicity by Walden, or the young man or woman who enters an abbey, or the couple who move to a farm in Vermont, or an Amish farmer hitching up his horses, or my friend who moved from a suburban house to a two-room apartment, giving away his entire library in the process, I realize that Thoreau, the novice, the couple, the farmer, and my friend are seeking not a mythical purity, but a genuine integrity. They are trying to live the life of their souls.

It is possible to do this in our day. It is possible for you, and it is possible for me. We can, if we seek it by degrees, find a simpler life lived out of the soul, God's center in us.

THERESE OF LISIEUX

SOME YEARS AGO when I knew even less than I know now, I bought a little paperback at a religious bookstore in downtown Boston, and I bought this book because I saw the name "Therese" on the cover. I'd always wanted to know more about Theresa of Avila, and on returning home I was disappointed to find that the book was about Therese of Lisieux, a Carmelite nun. I was even more disappointed when I read the book.

Born to a respectable middle-class family (her father was a watchmaker), Therese was a sickly child whose four older sisters became nuns. She entered the monastery at age fifteen. Her journal records her life there, her reactions, and then her slow death by tuberculosis. She died on September 30, 1897. She was twenty-four years old.

Her abbess published a cautiously edited version of her journal for circulation among French Carmelite houses, and word of Therese's piety spread through the country. Her journal was translated into many languages. People began to report her help in miracles of healing. In 1925 she was canonized. Later more complete editions of her journal appeared, some with photographs of her as a novice, nun, patient, and corpse.

I found her sayings saccharine and irrelevant to my concerns, but ten years later I came across Carol Flinders's fine collection of essays on saints, *Enduring Grace*, and read her chapter on Therese. Suddenly I saw Therese through Flinders's eyes. I saw a woman very different from the one I first encountered. Flinders showed me an intelligent woman—willful, sensitive, observant, and devoted to a life of prayer.

When Therese entered the abbey, most of the twenty other residents were women over fifty, and the abbess was an arbitrary, domineering, neurotic woman who swung between charm and abuse, depression and hysteria. It was hardly paradise. Therese was not surprised. She wrote in her journal, "I found the religious life to be exactly as I had imagined it."

The abbey was cold; the food was bad. Therese grew thin and she hated criticism, but when mildly admonished for breaking a vase she had not touched, she said nothing. When she began to cough blood, a sure sign of tuberculosis, a fellow nun remarked that life was sad.

Therese replied, "But life is not sad. If you had said 'The exile is sad,' I could understand. People make the mistake of calling what must end 'life,' but 'life' should only be used of heavenly things that will never end. . . . In this sense life is not sad. It is gay, very gay."

Shown a photograph of herself, she said, "Yes, but this is only the envelope. When will I see the letter?" She died after two months of terrible pain, but in ecstasy at the last. Her final words were "My God, I love you."

Therese of Lisieux is a puzzle to most of us alive today. She turned her back on everything we value and embraced a life that had not even minimal comforts and unreliable human company. Yet she seemed to find a peace in this unpeaceful community, a peace that most of us have not found with all our perks, vacations, summer homes, and air-conditioning.

Therese's journal, now titled *The Story of a Soul,* bears witness to this peace. Her feast day is October 3. She may be a puzzle to us, but she is one of our saints.

THE MYSTIC CABBIE

I WAS ON my way to the installation of the Reverend Thomas Shaw as bishop of the Episcopal Diocese of Massachusetts when I realized how late I was in leaving home. Halfway across the intersection of Beacon and Charles Streets in Boston, an empty cab came by, and I hailed it, got in, and said, "I want to go to the Boston University armory."

"No you don't," said the driver. "It's at the hockey rink."

I'm used to being recognized as a clergy person by my collar, but how did this guy know where I was headed? I didn't ask, but simply said "Okay."

He was a great bear of a man, somewhere north of fifty years old, with a great shaggy beard that was speckled with gray, gold-rimmed spectacles, and a mass of unruly hair.

"Look at the bumper sticker in front of us," he said as we drove down Beacon Street toward Kenmore Square.

"All I can see is the word *grace*," I replied.

"That's all you need to see," he said.

"You sound like a man of faith," I told him.

"Well, I'm kind of a mystic," he said. Then he paused. After a long wait, he continued: "You see, a few years ago, I heard a sound. It was all around outside of me. It was inside me too. It was like rushing water. It was like a roaring fire. It was like many multitudes. It was a voice, but it spoke no words. I heard this myself, and it changed my life."

The professional cleric in me wanted to take control of the conversation. I briefly considered asking him if this sound and wind could not have been the subway. But I saw the pointlessness of that question and quickly set it aside. Maybe this man was for real. Maybe his experience was true. I didn't know what to say, so I said nothing.

We pulled up to the hockey rink. Sure enough, there were flocks of priests and well-dressed laity pushing through the doors. I paid the driver.

He said to me, "There is only one miracle in the world, and that is when a father and mother lose their only child and do not curse God."

I had been right to listen to him. I looked into his face and smiled as if to say, "You said it." Then I headed in to watch the Holy Spirit descend on Bishop Shaw. But often during the installation, as beautiful as it was, I thought of the mystic cabbie.

There are still saints in this world. Sometimes we meet them.

THE LOVING QUESTION

You may have seen cars with a bumper sticker reading "Jesus Is the Answer." This has prompted some other bumper stickers, one of which says, "If Jesus is the answer, what is the question?" And another, briefer sticker reads simply, "The Question Is the Answer." If I were to enter into this bumper sticker dialogue, I would put on my car one that reads, "Jesus Is the Question."

When I read the gospels, I am struck with the number of questions that Jesus asks. I count sixty in Luke alone, questions, such as Who made me your judge? Do you think I have come to bring peace? Why do you call me good? Why don't you decide for yourselves? Why do you sleep? Why do you doubt? Why are you troubled?

Jesus asks more questions in this same gospel: Where is your faith? Is it lawful to do good on the Sabbath or not? If you love those who love you, what credit is that to you? Why do you call me Master and not do what I tell you? Who do people say that I am? Who do you say that I am? Do you love me? What do you want me to do for you?

Questions, questions, again and again. Like Socrates, Jesus pressed his listeners, critics, and disciples, the bored, the curious, the keen, the persistent, back against the wall, back into themselves with the questions that He put to them. Remember the lawyer who asked Him, "Who is my neighbor?"

Jesus answered him by telling the story of the Good Samaritan, but His story ended with a question. Jesus asked the lawyer, "Who was neighbor to the robber's victim?" and the lawyer answered, "The one who showed him kindness." Jesus said, "Yes. Go and do the same."

Do you see what happened here? The lawyer asked Jesus, "To whom *should* I show kindness?" And Jesus answered him with another question. "To whom *will* you show kindness?"

Like all great teachers, Jesus taught with questions, and he taught with questions because questions create a tension in us. We must respond to the query, and when we have responded, we resolve the tension that the question created. Jesus would not always satisfy His listeners with an answer. At times, of course, He did, many times. But sometimes He knew that they must become part of the dialogue, and then He queried them.

Jesus not only asked questions but was, I believe, Himself a question that God sent to push us from our fear and lethargy to make us respond, to make us realize that on this earth, we cannot be bystanders and observers. We ourselves must become the answer that God seeks from this earth. Jesus, by His very presence, made people face themselves, face the choice between adventure and safety, between generosity and selfishness, between a life that seeks life in death or a life that is already dead because it seeks to escape death. Jesus reminds us that to live is to choose.

A man who survived three years in Nazi death camps put this better than I can. In his book *Man's Search for Meaning*, Victor Frankl wrote, "We had to learn that it did not really matter what we expected from life, but rather what life expected from us. We needed to stop asking about the meaning of life and instead to think of ourselves as those who were being questioned by life— daily and hourly. Our answer must consist, not in talk or meditation, but in right action and right conduct."

That, I suppose, is what it means to be responsible, to be able to respond to the questions life puts to us when we face suffering, pain, and an uncertain future. To be human is to be able to answer, magnificently for a few, simply for most of us. Jesus is a question, but a loving question, a question who never doubts we have the power to answer. A question who trusts that our answers, however modest, will make their own contributions to humanity. That is the kind of question that gives us courage and reminds us that, even in our darkest hour, to be human is a noble fate.

THE ONE WHO SURPRISES

SAINT PAUL met Christ on the Damascus road in a blaze of light so bright that it blinded him for days, and in a voice that asked him, "Saul, why do you persecute me?"

The emperor Constantine met Christ in a vision of a cross in the sky above the battlefield with a legend, "In this sign you shall conquer."

Saint Martin met Christ in a beggar at the city gate of Tours. Julian of Norwich met Christ in a series of sixteen revelations. My friend Dan Wakefield met Christ in a shimmering halo. And I met Christ in a small collection of short stories about a Catholic priest and a Communist mayor who lived in a small town in the Po Valley.

The year was 1953 and I was twenty-one years old, a recent college grad, newly moved from the Midwest to Boston, a clerk at the U.S. Rubber Company on Atlantic Avenue near South Station, and as unhappy an agnostic as you might find drinking coffee on Sunday mornings in Harvard Square.

I had no interest in church or religious conversation, but for some strange reason, I picked up a book by an

Italian journalist, Giovanni Guareschi. It was called *The Little World of Don Camillo*. I bought it and read it, bought and read the next two in the series, and even saw a film based on these books starring a French actor named Fernandel.

And what struck me in this unlikely revelation? These were comic stories about a priest and mayor, out to beat and best each other. But there was something else. In each of the stories, Don Camillo, the priest, would at some point go into the church and speak to Christ above the altar. Although a consummate politician with his parish and in his village, the priest spoke to Christ with absolute honesty because Christ knew the truth about him. And Christ always answered him with humor and compassion. You could tell that Christ loved Don Camillo and would not let him get away with much.

I, who could barely stand to hear the word *God* in those days, was disarmed by these stories, and sometimes I felt as if I were standing before the altar, as if Christ were speaking to me.

That may be the point where I rediscovered Christ, or where Christ rediscovered me. It may seem strange to you that Christ should use short stories to reach a disillusioned graduate, but such is God's mercy and humility that he comes to us in whatever disguise will catch our attention.

Perhaps you know. Perhaps Christ came to you disguised and won you to his way. If so, you know that you are blessed.

THE PIETY OF ROOSEVELT

I CAN REMEMBER walking over to Donny Magarian's house on the day after Franklin Delano Roosevelt died, and when he came out of the house, Donny was crying. I couldn't believe it. I asked him why he was crying, and he said, "What's the matter with you? Don't you know the President's dead?" Well, sure, I knew the President was dead, but I didn't think that was any big deal. We were Republicans. Only in the years that have passed have I come to realize what a great man FDR was and why Donny Magarian had good cause to cry.

I was interested to read what FDR's most recent biographer said of him. Kenneth Davis confessed that he was at first put off by the offer of writing this biography. But as he began to look at FDR more closely, he became fascinated and finally decided to write the book. And it was the religious side of this Episcopalian that interested him the most. Davis writes,

> At the core of his conception of himself was the inward certainty that he was a chosen one of

the Almighty, his career a role assigned him by the author of the universe, and that the part he must act or play according to his best ability was a great one. Believing absolutely in God the Father and Jesus as the Son of God, believing that God was infinitely kind and good as well as all-wise and all-powerful, believing that history was a working out of divine purposes, he must and did believe that history was essential progress, from worse to better, inevitable because it was God's will.

Then Davis says, "As a chosen one, he himself was an instrument of progress, a special agent of divine beneficence, but only an instrument, only an agent." Thus Roosevelt "was required to seek great power, but he never did so with the feeling that he himself would become the power he exercised or even that it would become his personal property to be used in the service of his personal will. It remained assigned, imposed from on high. This conviction enabled him to act as if he were possessed of what Spengler called a dreamlike certainty of decision."

As I reflect on Davis's words about Roosevelt, he reminds me more and more of Lincoln, who also had to use great power at a time of crisis and yet who never made much of his own will. Lincoln once said, "I confess that in the long run I have been the object of events and not their master."

Roosevelt stands in contrast to the Axis leaders, particularly Hitler, who saw their own will as the reality that would shape history and control events. Perhaps sometime in years to come, Roosevelt will be remembered as a man who saw his place in history and who took that place as an act of obedience.

Roosevelt wrote a prayer that was later published in a small Unitarian collection called *Prayers of the Free Spirit:*

O God, our Father, make us worthy of the trust which Thou has placed in us. May we have bravery and devotion which befit these times. As a nation, may we have the warm courage of unity and the clear consciousness of seeking tried and precious moral values. As citizens, may we have the clean satisfaction that comes from the stern performance of our duty. May we have faith in the future of democracy and may we build for a world of lasting brotherhood and peace. Amen.

Franklin Delano Roosevelt died of a cerebral hemorrhage in Warm Springs, Georgia, on April 12, 1945. His last words were, "I have a terrific headache." Not great words perhaps, but he had said those already.

THOU HAST KNOWN ME

A FRIEND OF MINE once told me that what we have seen on our computer screens is absolutely nothing compared with what we'll see when personal computers can access not just the vast libraries of printed information available, but also the visual data that will come to us through countless cable television stations.

We will be able to sit in our studies at home, he told me, and have Bibles, encyclopedias, almanacs, commentaries, and heaven-knows-what come to the screen at the touch of our fingers. We can sit there and know just about everything. I almost heard the serpent say to Eve, "You will be like gods. You will know everything."

I suppose that's what the information game's about: knowing. Knowledge is power. And of course we must have power. We must have power because we know how things ought to go. All we need is the power to make things go that way. Therefore, knowledge. *Scio ergo sum.* I know, therefore I am.

But the snake knew, as Eve and Adam found out later, that there's a catch in every deal. And the catch of the information game is this: the loneliness of the knower. If all you do is know, you isolate yourself. You move away from the reality that you want to manage. You live in the Oval Office or on the top floor of the corporate tower or in an ivory tower or at the keyboard of your computer. You live in your mental world, which you try to inflict upon the world around you. You become lonely, and if you have power when you get lonely, you can do dangerous things. This is the consequence of knowing too much.

Laurens van der Post grew up as a child among the primitive peoples of Africa, and he said, "The most wonderful thing about primitive man is that wherever he goes in life he feels 'I am known.'"

Immediately I thought of Corinthians, the thirteenth chapter. "Then I shall know even as I am known."

That's what the Bible tells us. The person of faith believes: I am known. My lies, my deceptions, my self-deceptions, my acts of greed and aggrandizement, my cover-ups, and my excuses are known. Yet I am not rejected. Guilty, yes. Stupid perhaps. But rejected, cast off, tossed on the dung heap? No. I am known with all my sins, and all my loves known, my loyalties, my desires for good, my small efforts toward righteousness, all these too are known."

"O Lord, thou has searched me and known me," said the psalmist. "Thou knowest my downsitting and my uprising and understandest my thought afar off. I am known."

When you know you are known, you can face any pain, you can live every joy.

So, yes, here I sit at my computer screen, popping up little electric marks against a luminous gray screen and knowing that if I got a modem and a few software packages I could go on an information spree, a real bender. But I won't do that. What is more important is simply to sit sometimes in a corner and know that I and you are known, and to know that at any moment of the day you and I can turn our thoughts to God and know God loves us.

I'll take the computer as far as it takes me, and then I'll go with the primitives.

THE SCENT OF GOD

THE QUESTION seems impious. But as a child I knew that everyone had a smell. My mother smelled of lavender after her bath. My father smelled of sweat and pipe tobacco at the end of the day. My brother smelled of peanut butter coming out of the pantry. Everyone smelled, so why not God? And if so, what did he smell like?

The Bible tells us what God said and what he did and how he appeared as a cloud or a messenger (an angel), but why didn't it say how he smelled? I knew enough not to ask my aunts and uncles who would have thought me impertinent to raise that question.

When I came to Boston, I went to a wedding at a church where they burned incense, clouds of it, whole fog banks of myrrh and frankincense and heaven knows what else.

Incense was a metaphor for God, an olfactory symbol rather than a symbol seen or spoken. It's an ancient metaphor. Just as priests at a Catholic or Anglican liturgy swing the smoking censer around the altar or before the gospel or in circumambulation of the congregation, so their predecessors, the Levites in Jerusalem, burned incense on the sacrificial block of the high altar in the temple before they offered oxen, pigeons, goats, and lambs to the glory of God.

For many Christians, Hindus, and Buddhists, incense is the smell of the God. That won't do for all of us. Some of us go to nature for the smell of the holy. We go to the temple that God alone created, where we meet a different incense wafted from the mountains, forests, fields, and sea. There we are blessed with the pungent smell of pine, the heady smell of lilacs in the garden or orange trees in the orchard, the dark rich odor of the new-turned earth, the sweet and new-cut hay so intoxicating that we want to lie down and bury our faces in its fragrance, and even the good strong smell of manure, the dark life from which new life comes.

I can remember the smell of the air in early winter when I was a child, just before the first snow fell, a smell that still brings to me the excitement of sleds and snowballs, even though the snow in our town was never enough to hold a sled and the snowballs melted on formation. Smells sometimes more than sights and sounds can trigger the memory of a family dinner, a first love, or even a bombardment when the acrid odor of explosive filled the air.

So it's small wonder that smells may speak to us of an ineffable goodness in creation, an essential goodness that still is part of us and we are part of it.

We go to the woods, the sea, the shore, the garden, and the rivers to smell as well as to see that goodness and be refreshed in knowing it is there. For all of us, these ventures into creation are acts of prayer. Believers and nonbelievers know the uncreated goodness of our created world. Believers and nonbelievers alike are the stronger and better for having been there.

Blessed art Thou, O Lord our God, King of the Universe, who hast created sights and sounds and smells, wonders that witness to thy glory.

CONVERSATION WITH GOD

I ONCE READ an article about Jack Kornfeld, a teacher and practitioner of Buddhist meditation, which described what happened to him when he returned to the United States after living as a Buddhist monk for several years in Thailand. What happened, he said, was disaster: a string of broken relationships with women who left him because of his need and jealousy, and a near estrangement from his father who almost died in a serious accident and found his meditative son indifferent to his suffering.

"In retrospect," said Kornfeld, "I was pathologically detached. I wasn't feeling what it would mean to have my father die in front of me. . . . I didn't know if I was angry, sad, or happy. . . . I spent the next ten years using therapy along with meditation to reclaim my capacity to feel."

I found the same thing in a milder way. After five years of practicing centering prayer at home, I was bored. I was stuck in my relationship with God. I needed another practice, and that is when I began spiritual direction with a splendid Jesuit and in time began a different kind of prayer.

Since then I have talked to several people who took up prayer or some other spiritual discipline, either in place of or in addition to meditation. They told me that in their cases, not only did meditation not dissolve their rage or fear, but sometimes masked those feelings behind a guise of spurious calm and seeming peace. Only when they found their lives in turmoil despite their meditation did they realize that they needed to take another step on their spiritual paths.

We know simply from reading the newspapers that teachers of meditation, capable of deep contemplation, can use and abuse their own disciples and do this (like so many others) without any sense of moral failure. Meditation did not keep the head of the Naropa Institute and father of much Buddhist meditation in this country away from alcoholism and sexual misconduct. Meditation did not keep the director of Kripalu Institute from exploiting his disciples. But let me be clear. I speak of the limits of meditation, not its inherent faults.

Herbert Benson, who set up a marvelous meditation clinic at the Deaconess Hospital in Boston, suggests in his second book that meditation not only calms the body, mind, and soul, but also prepares them to attend to the next event. The purpose of meditation, he suggests, is preparation.

All I can say for myself is that the difference between sitting alone in meditation and sitting in relationship with God is the difference between night and day.

Meditation prepared me for my next step, and while I still meditate, it is the life of conversation with God that gives me life. And thus it has been with several of my friends.

I don't assume that this will be true for everyone. I assume that meditation is power on the path of prayer. But it's not the end of the path, and there are other powers and other ways of knowing God. My prayers came alive with conversation.

ACKNOWLEDGMENTS

THANKS TO RALPH HELVERSON, who asked me to take over his Sunday morning radio show in 1977; WCRB owner Ted Jones, who encouraged me despite my misgivings; the Vestry of King's Chapel, who paid the WCRB bills for twenty-two years; friends, colleagues, parishioners, and strangers, who provided me with stories, quotes, references, and the examples of their lives; Rich Higgins, who harassed me until I agreed to print these talks and who worked on them far beyond the call of duty; Skinner House Books, which wanted to publish them; and Faith, who kept me on track.